Language in Education:
Theory and Practice

TEACHING PRONUNCIATION: FOCUS on ENGLISH RHYTHM and INTONATION

by Rita Wong

A publication of   Center for Applied Linguistics

Prepared by   Clearinghouse on Languages and Linguistics

PRENTICE HALL REGENTS Englewood Cliffs, New Jersey 07632

Library of Congress Cataloging-in-Publication Data

Wong, Rita.
  Teaching pronunciation.

  (Language in education ; 68)
  "A publication of Center for Applied Linguistics."
  1. Language and languages--Study and teaching.
2. Oral communication--Study and teaching. 3. English
language--Pronunciation--Study and teaching. I. ERIC
Clearinghouse on Languages and Linguistics. II. Title.
III. Series.
P53.6.W66 1987   418'.007   87-11547
ISBN 0-13-895095-4

LANGUAGE IN EDUCATION: Theory and Practice 68

Office of Educational
Research and Improvement
U.S. Department of Education

This publication was prepared with funding from the Office
of Educational Research and Improvement, U.S. Department of Education, under contract no. 400-86-0019. The
opinions expressed in this report do not necessarily reflect
the positions or policies of OERI or ED.

Editorial/Production supervision: Martha M. Masterson
Cover design: Karen Stephens
Manufacturing Buyer: Lorraine Fumoso

Published 1987 by Prentice-Hall, Inc.
A Division of Simon & Schuster
Englewood Cliffs, New Jersey 07632

Printed in the United States of America

10 9 8 7 6 5 4 3 2

ISBN 0-13-895095-4 01

Prentice-Hall International (UK) Limited, London
Prentice-Hall of Australia Pty. Limited, Sydney
Prentice-Hall Canada Inc., Toronto
Prentice-Hall Hispanoamericana, S.A., Mexico
Prentice-Hall of India Private Limited, New Delhi
Prentice-Hall of Japan, Inc., Tokyo
Prentice-Hall of Southeast Asia Pte. Ltd., Singapore
Editora Prentice-Hall do Brasil, Ltda., Rio de Janeiro

Table of Contents

Language in Education: Theory and Practice

ERIC (Educational Resources Information Center) is a nationwide network of information centers, each responsible for a given educational level or field of study. ERIC is supported by the Office of Educational Research and Improvement of the U.S. Department of Education. The basic objective of ERIC is to make current developments in educational research, instruction, and personnel preparation readily accessible to educators and members of related professions.

ERIC/CLL. The ERIC Clearinghouse on Languages and Linguistics (ERIC/CLL), one of the specialized clearinghouses in the ERIC system, is operated by the Center for Applied Linguistics (CAL). ERIC/CLL is specifically responsible for the collection and dissemination of information on research and application in languages and linguistics and its application to language teaching and learning.

LANGUAGE IN EDUCATION: THEORY AND PRACTICE. In addition to processing information, ERIC/CLL is also involved in information synthesis and analysis. The Clearinghouse commissions recognized authorities in languages and linguistics to write analyses of the current issues in their areas of specialty. The resultant documents, intended for use by educators and researchers, are published under the series title, Language in Education: Theory and Practice. The series includes practical guides for classroom teachers and extensive state-of-the-art papers.

This publication may be purchased directly from Prentice-Hall, Inc., Book Distribution Center, Route 59 at Brook Hill Dr., West Nyack, NY 10995, telephone (201) 767-5049. It also will be announced in the ERIC monthly abstract journal *Resources in Education (RIE)* and will be available from the ERIC Document Reproduction Service, Computer Microfilm International Corp., 3900 Wheeler Ave., Alexandria, VA 22304. See *RIE* for ordering information and ED number.

For further information on the ERIC system, ERIC/CLL, and CAL/Clearinghouse publications, write to ERIC Clearinghouse on Languages and Linguistics, Center for Applied Linguistics, 1118 22nd St. NW, Washington, DC 20037.

Gina Doggett, Editor, Language in Education

Introduction

The teaching of pronunciation has fallen far behind that of other skill areas in meeting the communicative criteria that now guide second language instruction. In the past 15 years, studies of the language acquisition process have illuminated its complexities and have shown that the theoretical foundation for pronunciation teaching has been too narrow, not only in terms of its linguistic basis, but also in that it has not taken into account the degree to which the learner contributes to the language learning process. In the same 15-year period, both linguistic analysis and teaching methodology have undergone a shift in emphasis from a focus on form to an interest in function and meaning. However, pronunciation teaching methods and materials have been slow to respond to these developments. As a result, many teachers still believe that pronunciation teaching means teaching students to pronounce discrete sounds accurately.

While new designs for pronunciation teaching are needed, each new design faces greater scrutiny by a more sophisticated second language teaching professional community, which demands both theoretical justification and measurable accountability for any claims about instructional practices (Leather, 1985; Pennington & Richards, 1986). The renewed interest in the tenets of pronunciation is encouraging. In the meantime, teachers are looking for ways to help students develop comprehensible pronunciation. The few commercially available textbooks on the market (such as Morley, 1979; Gilbert, 1984; Prator & Robinett, 1985) cannot begin to meet the multifaceted needs of a large and diverse population of nonnative speakers. One alternative is for teachers to design their own materials and learning programs based on an updated view of teaching pronunciation so that more students could be served more immediately. This monograph is intended as a guide to support this effort.

The following assumptions underlie the orientation of this monograph:

1. pronunciation instruction should be learner-centered;

2. the goal of pronunciation teaching is to foster communicative effectiveness;

3. the level of communicative effectiveness depends on the learner, but in general, all learners need to be minimally intelligible; and

4. rhythm and intonation are the key elements of intelligibility in speech.

These assumptions are discussed in Brown, 1977; Morley, 1979; and Savignon, 1983.

The reader may be surprised to find that the monograph begins not with pronunciation exercises but with preliminary comments on preparing for pronunciation work. An instructional program that aims to be learner-centered must start with the learner and plan the syllabus on the basis of who the learners are and what goals they can reasonably achieve in the time allotted. The reader may also be taken aback by the absence of attention to work on individual sounds. This omission is deliberate. Such exercises are available in great abundance, and while most focus on minimal pairs, teachers have been able to adapt them to meet more communicative criteria (see for example Celce-Murcia, 1983). Teachers are asking for assistance with rhythm and intonation. To help meet this demand, this monograph devotes its full attention to these important features of pronunciation. This monograph is not intended to be a text but to guide teachers and to stimulate ideas to provide the seed for hundreds of personalized texts.

1
Preparing for
Pronunciation Work

Developing pronunciation in a second language is a complex and delicate process. Pronunciation, as one facet of language, is a form of behavior, but more than any other, it seems to expose an individual's sense of self. Moreover, for change to take place, the learner must first recognize a need for change. But the motivation for change, once recognized, can easily flag because the process is often too slow for impatient learners. Thus, measures to sustain this motivation must be built into the learning experience. These learning considerations are just as important as insight into the language itself.

Accounting for Learner Variables

Because learners vary perhaps as much as the types of possible learning contexts, these variables should be assessed before decisions are made about the learning program. A 5- or 10-year-old nonnative speaker immersed in a community of native speakers will have a greater potential for language acquisition without instruction than one whose classmates are predominantly nonnative speakers. A formally educated adult learner will bring cognitive abilities to the task that will be different from those of one who did not have a formal education and who may be nonliterate in the first language as well. A sophisticated language user, such as one who has had experience speaking more than one language, will approach the new pronunciation system differently from one whose total life experience has been with a single language. A learner whose exposure to English has been essentially through the written language and who has had limited opportunities to hear English spoken by native speakers will bring a set of assumptions about the pronunciation system that is different from that of a learner who has heard English natively spoken from the start. An adult at the beginning stages of language learning will have needs and abilities that are different from one who is at an intermediate or advanced level. These learner variables must be considered before decisions can be made about the approach to pronunciation instruction to be taken, the choice of materials and the kinds of adaptations to be made for any individual learner or group of learners. Unsatisfactory results are inevitable when the same approach and materials are applied to all learners regardless of background.

Motivating Learning

Motivation, essential in all learning, is clearly a factor in pronunciation success. However, motivating learners to develop their pronunciation is not easy. Concerns for pronunciation have often been overshadowed by the learner's need to get the ideas across, and pronunciation instruction that dwells on the microscopic features of language has been at odds with this objective. The emphasis on the precise articulation of individual sounds has also met with resistance from learners for various reasons. For example, some feel that if they were to produce these foreign sounds precisely, they would be losing a part of their own identity. Pronunciation learning also puts learners in a position of great risk: They risk making mistakes, being embar-

rassed, failing, and losing self-esteem. (For a more detailed discussion of risk-taking and language learning,
see Beebe, 1983.) Considering what learners face, it is
not surprising that pronunciation does not have a high
priority for many learners.

The teacher can and must play a large role in mold-
ing instruction not only to meet the objectives of language learners, but also to make this experience a posi-
tive one. What has not been altogether clear to students
(and teachers) is the connection between pronunciation
and communication. Learners need to know precisely
what this connection is, how well they are making the
connection, and what they need to do in order to im-
prove the connection. For example, before zeroing in on
the specifics of pronunciation, students must first experience using language as a tool for truly communicative purposes. The teacher can provide the setting and
stimulus for this communication experience, and help
analyze moments of communication breakdowns, some
of which can be inevitably traced to pronunciation difficulties. Once students recognize the role of pronunciation in the communication process, they are then ready
for focused pronunciation work.

In addition to accepting the reason for pronunciation work, students need to have an atmosphere of mu-
tual respect and trust in which to do this work. Here
again, the teacher's role is central. No textbook can
perform this function. Finally, teachers can promote
success by establishing clear, achievable objectives and
devising ways for students to take note of these achieve-
ments.

Identifying Realistic Objectives

Pronunciation work invariably suffers when students cannot relate it to their personal goals, feel threat-
ened by it, or have unrealistic notions of how quickly
progress can be made. Some students define as their
goal a specific score on a test, such as the Test of English as a Foreign Language (TOEFL). Because this particular test does not include a speaking task, some students consider the development of speaking skills to be

irrelevant. Other students see attempts to change their pronunciation as threats to their sense of self, or as attempts to change their personality. The likelihood of such a perception is greater when pronunciation lessons concentrate exclusively on perfecting specific sounds. Students are sometimes given no rationale for getting these sounds exactly right, and yet are made to feel bad for failing to do so. Still other students, and sometimes their teachers as well, underestimate the time and conscious energy that are required for pronunciation to change and develop.

Thus, productive pronunciation work depends on the identification of objectives that are relevant to and attainable by the students. Changing the students' pronunciation because it falls short of the norm is not a viable objective, but teaching students how to speak more clearly and effectively is. Dramatic changes in students' speech in 3 to 6 months are rare, but changes in their perception of speech phenomena in their own speech and that of native speakers can be significant. What can pronunciation instruction accomplish? It can:

1. show students the major components of the spoken English system;

2. demonstrate how these components contribute to the expression of meaning and to communication in general;

3. teach students how to perceive these features in natural speech;

4. teach students how to perceive these features in their own speech; and

5. give students tools to develop their pronunciation on their own.

By giving students specific means to develop independently, the responsibility falls on those who have the actual power to make the necessary changes.

Diagnosing Proficiency

An initial diagnosis of each learner's oral proficiency serves several purposes:

1. The individual attention personalizes the learning process from the beginning of the course and promotes motivation.

2. It helps the teacher identify areas of emphasis for the student. Most learners are unaware of or misapprehend their difficulties. The initial assessment can help them identify concrete examples of their strengths and weaknesses and focus their efforts during the course.

3. It helps the teacher select appropriate areas of emphasis for the class and make decisions about which lessons can be omitted or which lessons need elaboration.

Coupled with a second round of diagnoses at the completion of the course, these assessments also serve as a concrete measure of progress.

In selecting a diagnostic instrument, the following factors are considerations:

• how much time is required to administer it;
• how easy or difficult the results are to evaluate; and
• how much it tells you about students' pronunciation (and not about their inability to read, their problems with grammar, or their ability to organize information).

Possible diagnostic instruments include:

• an interview consisting of a set of questions asked of all students;
• a reading of a short passage or dialogue;
• a description of a series of pictures;
• completion of a task with another student (e.g., one student describes a figure and the other student makes a drawing according to the description);
• a listening task that taps into the student's percep-

tion of speech phenomena (e.g., stressed syllables, accented words, pitch contours; see Gilbert, 1984).

With the exception of the listening task, all the other diagnostics should be taped so that the teacher can evaluate them later.

Each type of instrument has its advantages and disadvantages. For example, the listening test can be given to a large number of students in one sitting. However, the students must be familiar with some of the linguistic vocabulary used, such as stressed syllables and pitch. In addition, the student's speech production can only be inferred from the test results. An interview elicits actual speech data, but if the student is hesitant to speak, the corpus will be too limited to make any kind of evaluation. If the test is too open-ended, allowing the students to choose to say only what they are comfortable saying, then the teacher is not able to identify what may be difficult for them. Tasks involving more than one student are confounded by dynamics between the two students that will affect the results. Task-based activities also take more time to do and to evaluate.

The use of reading texts as diagnostics has been criticized on the basis that oral reading and spontaneous speech are different processes and that a student who can read a passage well may speak poorly or vice versa. However, the advantages of using a reading are many, including the following: (a) the uniform database for every student facilitates the evaluation task for the teacher; (b) having a standard text eliminates the need to transcribe the students' speech samples, which would be necessary for the interview, the picture description, and the task-based activity; (c) the text can be controlled for length and level of difficulty, which students cannot avoid; and (d) the reading can be made more like a conversation by choosing a dialogue as the text. The teacher can take one part and the student the other, and then they can exchange parts. The teacher's participation makes it more enjoyable for the students and provides them with a sample of native-speaker speech that they can review as many times as they like.

Whatever diagnostic instrument is used, the data will have to be analyzed and interpreted for the students. Here is a suggested procedure for evaluating the data on the transcriptions of the students' speech:

1. Mark the points at which the student pauses with a slash (/); if the text is replete with these slash marks, the student needs work with thought groups.

2. Mark syllable lengths of one or two sample sentences (see Chapter 2 for a coding system that can be used); a student's tendency to pronounce syllables with equal timing can be easily demonstrated with this system.

3. Mark the words that come across as being prominent in one or two sample sentences (see Chapter 3). If students highlight too many words, it is difficult to determine where the main ideas are (e.g., *WHAT are WE going TO DO AFTER the BREAK?*). Students who highlight the wrong words (e.g., *The clock IS slow*) might come across as being argumentative.

4. Identify incorrectly stressed syllables (e.g., *anaLYsis* instead of *aNAlysis*).

5. Identify missing sounds or extra sounds (e.g., *It's a rounda building*). After making initial notes, try to organize the information into categories on a checklist (a sample is included in Appendix A). Listening for syllable length, accent, and pitch will be particularly difficult in the beginning and requires some training.

6. Identify the most glaring sound substitutions (e.g., *I fink* for *I think*).

The value of diagnosing individual students cannot be overemphasized. Some form of diagnosis, made manageable for the teacher, will make a significant difference in the students' performance in the course.

Need for a Systematic Approach

Pronunciation work can be implemented in a variety of ways. It might be the central and exclusive focus of the course. It might be a strand in a speaking or general language course. Its objectives may be explicitly articulated, desirable with older students, or implicitly carried out, recommended with young children. Whether explicit or implicit, effective pronunciation work must be systematic. A systematic approach emphasizes relationships among the parts of the system, such as the connection between syllables and rhythmic patterns; attention to one part supports the development of another. By identifying the key elements of the system, teaching priorities can be established, with elements playing critical roles receiving more attention than those playing lesser roles. On the basis of the overall system and the learner's individual needs and goals, the teacher can begin to plan the syllabus.

An unsystematic approach has rarely made an impact on learners. For example, one or two lessons may be given on the pronunciation of final *s* or *ed,* or a teacher may give lessons exclusively on so-called reduced forms. Such approaches have contributed to the feeling that pronunciation teaching is ineffective. A systematic approach also enables learners to acquire gradually a set of tools that will assist them in evaluating their own progress, a necessary ability for learners who wish to continue after class and once the course terminates.

Focused Listening Opportunities

Exposure to spoken English is important for pronunciation development, but exposure alone does not guarantee results. For many learners, it is focused listening that makes a difference. That is, learners need to know what it is they should be paying attention to; it might be the way a sound at the end of a word is connected to the sound at the beginning of the next word, for example. In planning the syllabus, be careful to provide sufficient samples of spoken English, according to the following criteria:

1. The samples should include texts that go beyond the sentence level—conversations, stories, explanations —sentences that are connected and are part of a whole with a beginning and an end.

2. Samples should include a range of participant roles: discourse among peers, among speakers of the same and opposite sex, among speakers of different ages and levels of authority.

3. Where possible, authentic speech should be included. The students' proficiency level is a determinant of the appropriateness of using authentic speech. If simplified or teacher-prepared language is used, it should be spoken as naturally as possible, and not distorted for the sake of artificial clarity.

The language classroom should be examined to determine to what extent supplementary language data must be supplied. Some classrooms are language rich, while others are language poor. An example of a language-rich class is one in which students hear a variety of speakers engaged in diverse communicative events. A language-poor classroom is one in which the students listen only to the teacher interacting with them as a teacher on classroom topics and tasks. Classrooms can be language poor even in an English-as-a-second-language (ESL) context. The criterion of a language-rich classroom is the quantity and quality of language that a learner can hear in that classroom.

Many sources of speech samples are available to be used for pronunciation work, including:

• commercially prepared tapes and videotapes that accompany grammar or listening comprehension texts;
• radio programs, such as National Public Radio's "All Things Considered" or Canadian Broadcasting Company's "As It Happens," or "Soundings";
• recordings of books;
• tapes of lectures (e.g., National Press Club, Commonwealth Club); and
• videotapes of television programs, plays, and films.

These sources provide the context in which the teacher can illustrate how features of pronunciation—stress, rhythm, and intonation—function in speech. One caution about using authentic examples is that they do not always follow the rules of pronunciation as they are commonly formulated in many traditional texts. Moreover, teachers who have not had experience analyzing stress, rhythm, and intonation will find it as difficult to apprehend as the students do.

Developing Effective Listening Skills

Although communication was long the tacit goal of language learning, language instruction rarely resembled the kind of communication that takes place beyond the classroom walls. Exercises did not require students to talk to or understand each other. Recognizing this deficiency, contemporary classrooms are attempting to make communication a priority. However, because these classrooms are composed of nonnative speakers of English, students need to understand other nonnative speakers and be understood by them if they are to engage in communication. Thus, students must first learn to be willing and effective listeners and speakers before they can focus on pronunciation in communicative contexts. An exercise to develop effective listening skills is described in the next section.

Developing a Comfortable Level of Fluency

In addition to a foundation in listening skills, students should have some experience of communicating with other students before focusing on the specifics of pronunciation. This experience helps tongue-tied students, or simply inexperienced speakers, who must labor tortuously to produce a few words. It is also beneficial for those who, because they lack communicative experiences, are unable to assess their degree of communicative clarity. Two kinds of exercises can be used for this purpose: the fluency workshop and the discussion. These are described in the exercise section that follows.

Exercises

These exercises require that the student command a corpus of vocabulary and syntactic structures sufficient to understand the directions and to speak spontaneously on a subject for at least 3 minutes.

Effective Listening Exercise

1. First explain that a communicative event includes at least one speaker and one listener, and that both affect the success of the event. Many people, whether they are speaking their native or nonnative languages, mistakenly believe that it is the speaker who bears the responsibility for the successful outcome of the communication. But listeners who fail to understand the speaker have a responsibility to ask for repetition or clarification. Moreover, if listeners do not show that they are listening, speakers may not be interested in continuing to talk. The way a listener exhibits listening behavior may vary from culture to culture. You will demonstrate an exercise to help the class focus on the listener's important role in communication. After the demonstration, the rest of the class will have an opportunity to take part.

2. Ask for a volunteer to come up to the front of the classroom and talk to you about a topic for 3 minutes. You will demonstrate listening behavior while the volunteer speaks. Ask the class to focus on you and to observe and record what you do as a listener to show that you are listening. You can ask the students to predict the kinds of behavior that they might see: for example, eye contact, listening sounds such as *uh-huh, mmhmm;* words such as *yes, yeah, oh?* and *really?;* and phrases asking for repetition and clarification. Try to be as natural as you can, and avoid exaggerating by using more listening behavior than normal.

3. At the end of 3 minutes, ask the class to enumerate what they observed. Ask the speaker to describe his or her feelings about your listening behavior and how they might have encouraged him or her to speak.

4. Now divide the class into groups of three, assigning each to one of the roles of listener, speaker, or observer. Suggest a couple of possible topics for the speaker to talk about, for example: describe your living accommodations, your trip to the United States, your current job, and so forth. Instruct the listeners to try to be most cooperative, to be attentive, to help the speaker by asking questions on the topic if the speaker seems to be at a sudden loss for words, but not to take over the talking. The observer should take notes of the listener's behavior and be ready to report to the small group when the speaker has finished talking. Allow 5 minutes for this part of the activity: three minutes for the speaker, and 2 minutes for the observer to report.

5. Ask one or two observers to summarize their observations for the large group. Then have the students switch roles: the observer becomes the listener; the listener becomes the speaker, and the speaker becomes the observer. Follow the steps outlined in No. 4.

6. For the final round, instruct the students to switch roles once again. The observer will become the listener, the listener becomes the speaker, and the speaker becomes the observer. Thus:

Round 1	Round 2	Round 3
S1—Speaker	S1—Observer	S1—Listener
S2—Listener	S2—Speaker	S2—Observer
S3—Observer	S3—Listener	S3—Speaker

7. After the students have played all three roles, spend about 10-15 minutes summarizing their observations of the activity. Start by making a master list of the ways listeners demonstrated effective listening skills. Then ask how the speakers felt. You might add these observations: (a) that the effective listener can obtain information from a speaker, even when the speaker may not be clear, by using good listening techniques, such as asking for clarification; and (b) that speakers can learn to be better speakers by being attentive to what listeners tell you they understand or do not understand.

This exercise establishes a common foundation for the class's understanding of what it means to communicate. However, you, as the teacher, need to assist the students by showing them when to use these techniques. Many students feel it is more polite to listen without understanding than to interrupt and get clarification. They need to be shown how to interrupt acceptably. The total time for this exercise, including the demonstration, is 45-50 minutes. (See Chan, n.d., for more information about this application of a counseling technique.)

The Fluency Workshop

This exercise, developed by Maurice (1983), gives the students a sense of improved fluency. It is a low-risk speaking task because it involves speaking to only one other person at a time, and no one monitors the conversation.

The idea of this exercise is to give students the chance to talk about the same topic but to three different listeners consecutively. They are given decreasing periods of time for each round. With each subsequent round, the speakers become more familiar with what they want to say and can say it more fluently. Allow 50 minutes for this exercise.

1. Ask the students to sit or stand in a large circle. (The first time around it is easier to have the students seated because the chairs help to identify locations when the students change partners).

2. Explain the purpose of the exercise—to develop the students' oral fluency by giving them three opportunities to talk about the same topic.

3. Explain the procedure. Pair students off and label one A and the other B. The As will begin as speakers; the Bs will begin as listeners. There will be three rounds. The first round will be four minutes long. Then the As will move one person to the right and speak on the same topic with a new partner for two minutes. For the third round, the As will again move one person to

the right and speak for one minute. (The times can be varied, but as an introduction to the exercise, shorter times work best.) The listeners should be reminded to use active listening behavior. They may ask questions to help the speaker continue speaking, but should not take over. Tell the listeners that you will be asking them to report on what they heard at some point. After the As have completed three rounds, the Bs become speakers and the As listeners. The As will nevertheless continue to move to new partners. Be sure the students understand what to do before you ask them to begin.

4. Give the speakers a topic; tell the Bs that they will have different topics, to prevent them from trying to use their listening time to prepare for their turn.

5. Begin the exercise. It will be noisy, because half the class will be speaking simultaneously. The buzz may warm the hearts of teachers who want to encourage students to speak, but neighboring classes may not share the same enthusiasm, so make appropriate arrangements.

6. After the As have finished, ask a few Bs to report on what they heard. Then give the Bs their topic.

7. After the Bs have finished, ask some of the As to report on what they heard.

8. When both As and Bs have concluded their three turns each, ask students to discuss any differences they could detect between the first and third rounds. They will generally say that it was easier for them to talk about the same thing on the third try.

This exercise can be used as many times as the class likes during the course.

The Discussion

Students who have had little or no prior experience with discussions in their previous schooling may not appreciate the importance that teachers in the United States place on discussions. An orientation to discussion as a teaching and learning tool helps to inform and alter their view. The next step is to initiate the students in what may be their first discussion experience. You can facilitate this experience by making the structure of a discussion explicit and by defining the roles of the participants. Following is a procedure for doing so.

1. Decide on a topic. To begin, choose a topic that every student can easily say something about, such as: "Think of as many ways to keep warm as you can," or "What can you do to study for the TOEFL?"

2. Determine the composition and size of each group. Aim for heterogeneity of language backgrounds, personalities, and language abilities. Groups of between four and six students work well. As students warm up to discussions and the composition of each group is of less significance, an easier and faster way to divide students up is to count them off by fours if you want four groups, fives if you want five, and so on. Other ways to divide students are: early risers/late sleepers; oldest/ middle one/youngest in a family; those who wear glasses and those who don't; and so on.

3. Assign and explain the roles of participants in a discussion. These roles have been prescribed in order to teach students about discussions, since many have not had experience with them.

   a. The *discussion leader* is responsible for introducing the topic, making sure that everyone understands it, and making sure everyone in the group has a chance to speak—that no one person monopolizes the discussion and that reticent students are encouraged to contribute.

   b. The *reporter* takes notes of what participants say during the discussion and summarizes these comments for the larger group at the conclusion of the small group discussion. The reporter also participates in the discussion.

   c. The *participants* listen actively by asking for clarification, checking for understanding, and adding comments to the topic.

4. Establish a time limit for the small-group discussions and make sure everyone knows what the time limit is.

5. Check to be sure that the group leader understands what the topic is.

6. When time is up, listen to the reports from each group. Plan the class hour so that there is time for this part of the discussion exercise.

7. Comment on the way the discussions were carried out, as well as on the reports. Your comments will depend on the objectives of the particular discussion.

During the discussion, the teacher can circulate among the groups, listening and participating only when asked and then only to answer a specific question briefly. Keep in mind that the discussion exercise is an opportunity for the students to speak.

These three activities—the effective listening exercise, the fluency workshop, and the discussion—serve important functions as preparation for pronunciation work. By gaining immediate and direct experience as communicators, learners can see the need for developing their own intelligibility. By acquiring a few tools to get started as communicators, they will be able to make the best use of the communicative activities that teachers provide in the classroom. These activities can and should be recycled throughout the course, interwoven with the focused pronunciation exercises, each supporting the other.

2

The Rhythm of English

What Should Be the Focus of Pronunciation Teaching?

A common-sense view of speech production, supported by the tenets of the audiolingual method, maintains that clarity depends on the correct pronunciation of the individual sounds of a language. However, contrary to this concept, contemporary views hold that the sounds of a language are less crucial for understanding than the way they are organized. The rhythm and intonation of English are two major organizing structures that native speakers rely on to process speech. Not only do rhythm and intonation provide structure, but they also direct the listener to the centers of attention in the stream of speech. Moreover, intonation, as a form of linguistic gesture, plays an important role in the establishment and maintenance of social harmony (Wong, 1986).

Because of their major roles in communication, rhythm and intonation merit greater priority in the teaching program than attention to individual sounds. In addition, since students usually have a limited time frame for formal language study, as a matter of expedience, they should work on the features of pronunciation that have the greatest bearing on communicative effectiveness. This is not to say that the pronunciation of individual sounds is irrelevant, but that it is neither automatically the starting point nor the focus of learning to speak a language. For the general language learner, the payoffs are greater when sounds are treated within the framework of rhythm and intonation: The learner does not have to make the transition from learning the forms of sounds in isolation to learning their forms in the stream of speech. Moreover, within this framework, the sounds that will receive the greatest attention will be the ones that preserve rhythm and intonation, for example, the vowels and word-final and word-initial sounds—both vowels and consonants. Although rhythm and intonation are interrelated, they are presented in separate chapters for the purposes of discussion. Intonation is the subject of the next chapter.

What Is Rhythm?

The rhythm of English is one of the most difficult features for nonnative speakers to learn and for native speakers to unlearn when studying other languages. The rhythm of a language is characterized by the timing pattern of successive syllables. In many languages other than English, every syllable is given about the same length. By contrast, English syllables vary in length; a word may be composed of a sequence of a short syllable followed by a long syllable and a short syllable, as in the word *successive*. This variation is typical at the sentence level as well, although sentences with monobeats, that is, monosyllabic words of equal length, can be found. An example is the farewell given by an astronaut to a satellite he had just repaired: *There that bad boy goes.* Because sentences composed of monobeats are atypical in English, they call attention to themselves. Compare *Now hear this!* with one beat per word to *Listen to this!* with two beats of unequal time in the first word. The former with its monobeats carries a greater sense of urgency than the latter.

It is not uncommon for learners unconsciously to impose the rhythmic patterns of their native language on the new language, unaware that rhythm is a variable in either the native or target language. As a consequence of applying monobeats to English, nonnative speakers sometimes unwittingly draw abnormal attention to what they say, even being mistakenly perceived to be insistent. Aside from the hazard of being misjudged, not knowing the rhythmic system of English is likely to interfere with communication in general because, as was mentioned earlier, rhythm is an organizing principle of speech. Causing even more difficulty for the learner is the fact that the features of rhythm are not represented in the writing system.

The key to the rhythmic system of English is syllable length, which is affected by the following five factors:

1. *Stress.* Stressed syllables are longer than those that are not; stressed syllables are those that are marked in the dictionary as stressed.

2. *Accent.* Accented syllables are longer than those that are not; accented syllables are the ones that are made prominent by the intonation contour.

3. *Vowel Type.* Full vowels are longer than reduced vowels. In Bolinger's (1981) analysis of vowel types, there are three reduced vowels: the mid-central vowel /ə/, also known as schwa; the front vowel / ɨ /, which is the final sound found in some speakers' pronunciation of the word *city;* and the back vowel / ɵ /, which is the final sound found in some speakers' pronunciation of the word *potato.* Differentiating three reduced vowels may be too difficult for both students and teachers, particularly when the front and back reduced vowels are not typically found in the teachers' dialect. Moreover, the front and back reduced vowels are not represented as such in citation forms in the dictionary. Thus, for practical, rather than linguistic considerations, concentrate on /ə/, because it is the most identifiable reduced vowel. The main point is that the reduced vowel should be pronounced with a relaxed tongue and lips and more quickly than a full vowel.

4. *Syllable Structure.* Syllables may end in a consonant (a closed syllable) or a vowel (an open syllable). An open syllable is longer than a closed syllable. In closed syllables, length is also conditioned by the nature

of the consonants, whether they are voiced or voiceless, stops or continuants: Compare *goat,* which ends in a voiceless consonant, and *goad,* which ends in a voiced consonant. Closed syllables ending in voiced consonants are longer than those ending in voiceless consonants. Closed syllables that end in continuants (e.g., /m, n, f, v, w, r, s, z/) are longer than those that end in stops (e.g., /p, t, k, b, d, g/). For example, compare *glows* and *globe.*

5. *Pauses.* Pauses should generally occur at phrasal boundaries as opposed to at the end of every word or even at the end of syllables within a word.

All five of these factors will be illustrated in this chapter and the next.

Introducing English Rhythm

Rhythm is familiar even to the youngest child beating on a table with a spoon. It can be heard in a swimmer's strokes or those of a tennis player, and of course, in poetry and music. But rhythm in language is less familiar because it is less obvious. With young children, music, rhymes, and storytelling can be exploited for their wealth of rhythmic examples without resorting to explicit treatments of the phenomenon. Adult learners, however, will benefit from conscious attention to the features of rhythm: syllable length, stressed syllables, full and reduced vowels, pauses, linking and blending sounds between words, and how words are made prominent by accenting syllables and simultaneously lengthening syllables.

Begin by helping students make the connection between rhythm in general and the rhythm of language in particular. For example, take a song with a simple rhythmic pattern and ask students to tap their toes, clap their hands or nod their heads as you sing or play a recording of the song. Malvina Reynolds' "Little Boxes" works well for this purpose. Call the students' attention to the syllables and words that fall on the beat, which take up more time than the syllables and words between the beats. While spoken English does not have the regularity of rhythmic beats as songs and poems do, the timing principle is the same. Ask students to listen to expressions such as the following and to try to identify where the heavy beats fall:

1. How's it going?
2. Let's take a break.
3. Let's call it a day.

In (1), the heavy beats fall on *how's* and *go;* in (2) on *let's* and *break;* and in (3) on *call* and *day.* These words take longer to say, while the other words are spoken more quickly.

A nonmusical way of introducing rhythm is to select a taped conversation, one that realistically represents language in use and is a good illustration of the rhythm of a conversation as well as the rhythm of language (the tapes by Richards & Bycina, 1984, satisfy these criteria). Identify the heavy beats in the conversation so that you can tap them out for the students. Once introduced to this dimension of language, the students will become sensitive to its features and can begin to explore its properties.

Teaching Syllable Length

The heart of the rhythmic system—syllable length—may be initially difficult for students to apprehend through the ear but may be more clearly demonstrated through the use of the other senses. Getting students to feel differences in length through body movements, or kinesthetics, is one avenue. The use of rubber bands or other elastic materials for this purpose was introduced by Gilbert (1978). By stretching the rubber bands to correspond with the length of syllables, students can feel the difference in a concrete manner. You can also exploit the sense of sight by showing length as a set of lines or circles:

	Circles	Lines
short	.	-
long	o	—

Circles marked over syllables are generally easier to see than lines, and for this reason are used here. While there are more than two degrees of syllable duration in speech, two seems a practicable number for the purpose of demonstrating the concept of syllable length variation. The small dot identifies a syllable of short duration. The circle identifies a syllable of comparatively longer duration. While pitch is also a variable in what is perceived by English speakers as lengthened, for the moment it suffices to note that when you pronounce the words and phrases, some students will hear pitch along with syllable length and reproduce it as well. Using this system, the rhythm of the word *banana* is represented as follows:

.   o   .
ba na na

Exercises

To introduce students to the concept of differences in syllable length, try the following exercise.

Introductory Exercise on Syllable Length

1. Take a set of three-syllable words, such as *bananas, pineapples, oranges, apricots,* or *computer, monitor, Macintosh, IBM.* Mark the syllable lengths of each word and ask students to note the differences in length as they listen to you read each one. The list could be written on the board or on handouts. For nonliterate students, choose items that you can bring in. You may want to practice reading these words, checking to be sure that they are read naturally, without undue clarity or speed.

```
  .  o  .              .    o  .
 bananas               computer

  o   o  .             o  .  .
 pineapples            monitor

  o   .    .           o  .  o
 oranges               Macintosh

  o   .  o             o o o
 apricots              IBM
```

2. Before the second reading, distribute rubber bands to each student (the wider, the better). Ask the students to hold them with the index finger of each hand and practice stretching the rubber bands: a little and a lot.

3. Show the students how to stretch the rubber bands to correspond with the length of a syllable. Try it with *banana.* They should stretch the band a little for *ba,* more for *na,* and a little again for *na.* Exaggerate on the longer syllable: stretch—S T R E T C H—stretch.

4. Continue with the rest of the words.

5. Now ask the students to pronounce each word with you as they stretch the rubber bands.

6. Divide the students into pairs to practice, and go around to listen and watch as they do.

In choosing your list of words, think of topics of particular interest and relevance to your students: words they need to use, words they will come across frequently, words they are learning in other classes, words that are fun. Epstein (1983) asked his students to think of words that described a person whom they are or have been in love with, and used those words for work on vowel length.

Example Practice Exercise: Syllable Length

After students have been introduced to the idea of contrasting syllable length, they need opportunities to listen to these contrasts in the ordinary use of language. The word *potato* is a good example of contrasting syllable length: short-long-short. In the following text, the word *potato* is used 14 times in an uncontrived and interesting way.

The Potato Museum

Did you know that there is such a thing as a potato museum? Well, there is. It's in Washington, D.C. The museum shows the evolution of potato cultivation from the use of early hoes to the modern potato combine, a machine that harvests potatoes. It also shows how the cultivation of the potato began in Peru and Bolivia and was later introduced in Europe by the Spanish Conquistadors. North America got the potato from Bermuda and the English colonists. The museum's displays include potato poems, songs, stories, jokes *(What has eyes but can't see?)*, recipes and even postage stamps. On the museum's poster is this comment from Louis Pasteur, "Curiosity and interest are immediately aroused when you put into a young person's hands, a potato." A reproduction of Van Gogh's painting, "The Potato Eaters," is in the museum, along with his comment, "I have tried to make it clear how these people, eating their potatoes under the lamplight, have dug the earth with those very hands they put in the dish and so it speaks of manual labor, and how they have honestly earned their food." In the U.S. today, four kinds of potatoes can be found: round white, long white, round red (commonly called "new" potatoes) and Russet. Long whites and Russets can be baked, mashed or fried. Round reds are the best for potato salad. Any of the four types can be used for soups and stews. Did you know the potato has such a history?

This text provides opportunities for students to listen for the contrasting lengths in the word *potato* many times and subsequently to use it in talking about the text. Repetition is built into the text in a natural rather than a mechanical way. One procedure for using this text is outlined below.

1. Read the text (or have someone with a different voice quality, e.g., male if you are female or vice versa, on tape) and ask the students to listen for the overall meaning.

2. For the second reading, ask the students to count the number of times they hear the word *potato* or *potatoes,* noting the contrasting syllable lengths.

3. For the third reading, ask students to listen with the objective of retelling the text to another student, pronouncing the word *potato* with the short-long-short pattern each time they use it.

Before the students produce their own versions of the text, they will have heard the rhythm of *potato* 42 times, the first 14 times without explicit attention to the form of the word, the second 14 times focused on it, and the last 14 times unfocused on it. In retelling the text, the intent is twofold: to help students learn to monitor themselves, beginning with the one word, and to initiate students into contrasting syllable length.

Stressed Syllables and Syllable Length

Stressed syllables, as marked in the dictionary, are longer than those that are not. Pitch changes also occur on stressable syllables, but pitch will not be formally introduced at this point. Students who can use the dictionary to find the stressed syllable(s) of a word in a dictionary will have a tool they can turn to long after the class has ended. In the following exercise, students are asked to identify the primary stressed syllable. In selecting words for this exercise, include only those with one stressed syllable marked. A second sample dictionary exercise on "secondary" stress follows.

Using the Dictionary to Find the Stressed Syllable of a Word. Dictionaries contain information that will help students pronounce words. One important piece of information is the primary stressed syllable, which is the longest syllable of a word (there may also be a change in pitch on this syllable, but this is not of concern at the moment). It identifies a word as much as the sounds of the word do. If a speaker places the stress on a syllable other than the one marked in the dictionary, the listener may have difficulty identifying which word it is, or if it is an English word at all.

First, look up selected words in your dictionary. Note the system used by your dictionary to mark the primary stress. It will be marked in one of the following three ways:

1. before the stressed syllable   'dic tion a ry

2. after the stressed syllable   dic' tion a ry

3. over the vowel of the stressed syllable   díc tion a ry

Your dictionary will also show a "secondary stress," typically below the letter, either just before or just after the syllable. Ignore this mark for now. Its function will be studied in the next exercise.

Mark each of the words in the following way: mark the stressed syllable with a circle and the rest of the syllables with a dot. For example:

$$\begin{array}{cc} o & . \\ \text{sur} & \text{face} \end{array}$$

$$\begin{array}{ccc} o & . & . \\ \text{vi} & \text{ta} & \text{min} \end{array}$$

$$\begin{array}{cccc} . & o & . & . \\ \text{in} & \text{tel} & \text{li} & \text{gent} \end{array}$$

(Choose words that will be interesting and useful to your students and do not have secondary stress.) After the students have marked these words, they can show how the syllables differ in length using a rubber band. Then they can practice pronouncing the words with a partner.

You can devise a series of dictionary exercises focusing on stressed syllables to be used throughout the semester.

A Second Dictionary Exercise. Turning to "secondary stress," recall that for the word *dictionary*, a second mark appears below the letter, either before or after the syllable. This mark provides two pieces of information: (a) the vowel in that syllable is a full vowel, in other words, it is not one of the "swallowed vowels"; and (b) you would give some length to this vowel. However, no pitch changes will occur on this syllable.

Look up the following words and mark both the primary-stressed and the secondary-stressed syllable with a circle; mark the remaining syllables with a dot.

```
o  .  o
analyze
```

```
o     .    o
neighborhood
```

```
o    o     .
programmer
```

After students have been introduced to pitch changes in the next chapter, you can return to this exercise and show them how pitch changes occur only on the primary-stressed syllable.

Full and Reduced Vowels and Syllable Length

Reduced Vowels. The nature of the vowel is another influence on syllable length. The duration of reduced vowels is shorter than that of full vowels. A word such as *banana* is composed of a sequence beginning with a reduced vowel, followed by a full vowel, then a reduced vowel:

ba	**na**	**na**
reduced	full	reduced
short	long	short

The rhythm of *banana* is short-long-short. One way to think of reduced vowels is in their manner of production: The lips are not as tight or tense, the tongue more relaxed than when the full vowels are pronounced. The most common reduced vowel is represented in the dictionary as /ə/, called schwa. When you see this symbol, you know the vowel is reduced and therefore short. Note that the term short refers to the duration of the vowel and not to the conventional names of vowel letters in reading instruction.

Show the students how to pronounce this vowel by contrasting it with the three basic vowels: / i / as in *tea,* /u/ as in *two,* and /a/ as in *father.* Draw a picture of the mouth and show how the tongue tip moves forward for

/ i /, back for /u/, and the jaw is lowered for /a/.

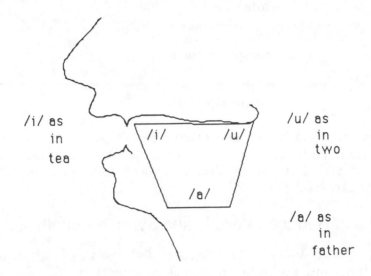

The Three Basic Vowels Contrasted with Schwa

Have the students repeat the three vowels after you: /i/, /u/, and /a/. Ask them to feel the tongue move forward for /i/ and back for /u/. Have them say these two or three times so they can sense the difference: /i/-/u/; /i/-/u/; /i/-/u/. Point out the definite shape of the lips for /i/—they're spread—and for /u/—they're rounded.

Now compare /i/ and /a/. Say these two or three times: /i/-/a/; /i/-/a/; /i/-/a/. Note again the spread lips. Do the same for /u/ and /a/. Note the rounded lips for /u/ and the unrounding for /a/.

Now pronounce the word *another*. The first vowel in this word is the reduced vowel, schwa /ə/. Ask the students to say *another* two or three times and try to sense where the tongue is and how it feels at the beginning of the word. The tongue is neither high nor low, front nor back, but in the middle. It is also relaxed. The shape of the lips is neither spread nor rounded. Because of these characteristics, the vowel schwa cannot be as clearly perceived as the other vowels.

Give the students an opportunity to listen and watch

as you pronounce a list of two-syllable words that have the reduced vowel schwa in either the first or second syllable. Have the students number from one to 10 on a sheet of paper. For each word they hear, they should write *1st* or *2nd* according to whether the schwa is in the first syllable or the second. Here is a possible list:

1.	agree	(1st)
2.	college	(2nd)
3.	conclude	(1st)
4.	mama	(2nd)
5.	receive	(1st)
6.	untrue	(1st)
7.	reduce	(1st)
8.	poppa	(2nd)
9.	believe	(1st)
10.	opera	(2nd)

Notice that the word *opera* may be pronounced as two or three syllables. Determine how you pronounce this word. If you pronounce it as three syllables, delete it from the list.

Then check the students' responses. Next, write these words on the board and indicate the reduced vowel by drawing a slash mark through it. Call the students' attention to the fact that no one vowel letter represents this sound. In these examples, the reduced vowel is represented by: *a, e, o,* and *u.* Practice pronouncing these words, concentrating on making the reduced syllable shorter.

Dictionary Exercise: Identifying the Reduced Syllable Schwa. In addition to providing information about stressed syllables, the dictionary also identifies the reduced syllable, schwa. This exercise shows students how to use the dictionary to find this information.

Look up the following words in your dictionary. Write the schwa symbol over the appropriate letters. For example:

ba na na

com pu ter

$$\overset{\scriptsize\vartheta}{\text{sur face}}$$

$$\text{break f}\overset{\scriptsize\vartheta}{\text{a}}\text{st}$$

$$\text{vow }\overset{\scriptsize\vartheta}{\text{e}}\text{l}$$

$$\text{syl l}\overset{\scriptsize\vartheta}{\text{a}}\text{ b}\overset{\scriptsize\vartheta}{\text{l}}\text{e}$$

$$\text{en v}\overset{\scriptsize\vartheta}{\text{e}}\text{ lope}$$

Continue the list with words of relevance to your students. After the students have marked the vowel pronounced as schwa, have them mark the length of each syllable using the circle system. Then ask the students to practice pronouncing the words, concentrating on making the distinctions in syllable length as shown.

Full Vowels. A simple way to differentiate between full and reduced vowels, following Gilbert (1984), is to describe full vowels as those that are clearer than reduced vowels. When students (and native speakers, too) miss hearing syllables in a word, these are usually the reduced vowels (e.g., a student may hear *mometer* for *thermometer).* Following is a sample exercise for students to gain practice listening for full vowels.

Full and Reduced Vowels Exercise. Notice what happens to the clarity of the vowels of the words in the first column when they occur in unstressed syllables in the second. Look these words up in the dictionary and write the symbol for the underlined vowel in the spaces provided.

face	___	surface	___
break, fast	___	breakfast	___
gage	___	baggage	___
land	___	Oakland, England	___
man	___	salesman	___

ch<u>a</u>se	___	purch<u>a</u>se	___
m<u>ou</u>th	___	Plym<u>ou</u>th	___
f<u>ou</u>nd	___	Newf<u>ou</u>ndland	___
r<u>a</u>te	___	separ<u>a</u>te	___
c<u>a</u>n	___	Americ<u>a</u>n	___
f<u>o</u>rd	___	Medf<u>o</u>rd	___
f<u>o</u>rt	___	eff<u>o</u>rt	___
s<u>a</u>nd	___	thous<u>a</u>nd	___

Relative Syllable Length

In addition to stress and vowel type, syllable length is influenced by its structure: open or closed, and the type of consonants that close or end a syllable. As pointed out earlier, syllable length is a central feature of rhythm. In addition, it also plays a role in word identification. Some students have difficulty making distinctions between words that differ only in their final consonant sound, such as the difference between *bet* and *bed*. Some pronunciation texts attempt to help students by focusing the difference between the final consonants. However, perceptual studies show that it is the length of the preceding vowel that listeners use to identify the word. This finding suggests that exercises focusing on vowel length would be more productive. The following exercise serves simply to focus the students' attention on syllable length. It is not necessary for students to identify the differences in length among the intermediary words, only that the vowel lengths increase from relatively short to relatively long as you read from left to right. You can use the rubber bands to show length here as well. Have the students listen and stretch their rubber bands along with you as you read. Then have them say these words after you and try to make each subsequent vowel longer. Although the length differences are small, asking students to make them longer draws their attention to a feature they may not have noticed before.

Short				Long	
wait		weighed	ways	Wayne	weigh
weight		wave			way
grate	grace	grade	graze	grain	gray
great			grays		
plate	place	played	plays	plain	play
seat	cease	seed	seas	seen	sea
			seize	scene	see

Relative Syllable Length Exercise No. 1. The following exercise gives students an opportunity to listen to pairs of words and compare the vowel lengths in each. Read each pair twice: Read the first word followed by the second, and then read the second word followed by the first. This way they will hear each word read with both intonation patterns.

Instructions to the student: Listen as your teacher reads pairs of words. Decide which vowel is the longer of each pair. For example, in the first pair, *way* and *weight,* which vowel is longer, the one in the first or the second word? (the first). On your answer sheet, circle first or second, according to what you hear.

The student worksheet would look like this:

1.	first	second	
2.	first	second	*etc.*

The teacher's key for this exercise would look like this:

1.	way	weight

2.	great	gray
3.	play	played
4.	seed	sea
5.	plain	plate
6.	weight	wave
7.	graze	great
8.	played	plain
9.	seen	seed
10.	seas	cease

Relative Syllable Length Exercise No. 2. This exercise is more difficult because the contrast in length is not as great as it is in the words in the first exercise.

1.	weighed	weight
2.	graze	grace
3.	place	plays
4.	seed	seat
5.	plate	played
6.	grays	grace
7.	place	plays
8.	cease	seas
9.	seats	seeds
10.	grades	grates

Relative Syllable Length Exercise No. 3. Now that students have had a chance to compare syllable length in pairs of isolated words, they can move on to listening for the same differences with the words embedded in sentences. In the next exercise, an adaptation of a procedure developed by Bowen (1972), students will listen for as well as try to say these words with enough differentiation in syllable length so that listeners can distinguish one sentence from the other.

Begin by demonstrating the meaning of the following pairs of exchanges created by Gilbert (1984):

Speaker A: There's something in my eyes!
Speaker B: Call a doctor!

Speaker A: There's something in my ice!
Speaker B: Call a waiter!

Point out to the students that the main difference between *eyes* and *ice* is that the vowel in eyes is longer than the vowel in ice. (Clueing students in to this difference is much more effective than to the voicing difference between the two final consonants). Now ask them to take Speaker B's part. If you say *There's something in my eyes!"* they should respond with *Call a doctor!* and if you say *There's something in my ice!* they should say *Call a waiter!* Try it with the class a couple of times. Then ask individual students to respond as you say either sentence.

The practice session can be organized in one of two ways, depending on the size of your class. If you have a small class (up to 20), you can arrange the students into a circle. Then tell the students that each person will have a chance to try saying the two sentences, and class members will respond according to what they hear. You will tell the students which sentence to say by raising one finger for sentence one and two fingers for sentence two. Stand behind one of the students in the circle. This student will be Speaker B. The student opposite will be Speaker A. You will signal to this student which sentence to say. In this way, everyone but the respondent will know which sentence Speaker A will attempt to say. After these two students have had several turns, move to the next person in the circle, who will be the new Speaker B. The new Speaker A will be the person opposite.

If you have a large class, or if the classroom is fixed so that a circle arrangement is impractical, ask the student who will be Speaker A to go to the front of the room facing the students. You can signal this student from the back of the room. Class members may be designated as Speaker A and B in some prearranged order. In this setup, only Speaker A will know which sentence he or she is attempting to say following the teacher's signal.

Another minimal dialogue pair:

A: Have you seen a cap?
B: There's one on the table.

A: Have you seen a cab?
B: There's one across the street.

The following conversation might take place in a car:

A: Can you put my glasses in the back?
B: Pass them over.

A: Can you put my glasses in the bag?
B: The brown ones?

You can also make up your own to use throughout the semester, since students will benefit from continual attention to syllable length.

At this point, students know the following points:

1. English words are composed of syllables that vary in length.

2. Every word of more than one syllable has a primary-stressed syllable that is longer than the other syllables in the word, and this stressed syllable is marked in the dictionary.

3. Vowel type determines syllable length. Full vowels are longer than reduced vowels. The spelling system does not distinguish full vowels from reduced vowels. However, the dictionary identifies one of the reduced vowels with the symbol /ə/. The others must be determined by ear.

4. Syllable structure affects syllable length.

Students can now begin a set of practice exercises that start by teaching them to use a marking system that indicates how to read a text with the rhythm pattern of English. After they have learned to read the marked text, they rehearse the same text until they can produce it without reading. For longer texts, the "Read and Look Up" technique can be used (West, cited in Via, 1976). Students may look at the text, but when they are ready to speak, they must look up and make eye contact with their listeners while they are speaking.

Reading Marked Syllable Length Exercise No. 1. In this exercise, which simulates a real conversational interchange, students working in pairs begin by practicing asking the meaning of and explaining abbreviations, focusing on syllable length. Each syllable is coded for length with a dot for a short syllable and a circle for a long syllable so that the students have a visible check on how long each syllable should be. If students do well, you can try having them come up with their own abbreviations for their partners to query them about.

A. What do the following abbreviations mean?

    o o o   o o .   o . . o . .
1. USA   (United States of America)

    o o o   o o o . o . .
2. NYU   (New York University)

    o o o   . o . .   o o .   o   . .
3. ABC   (American Broadcasting Company)

    o o o o   o . o . . . o . o . . o o . .
4. UCLA (University of California at Los Angeles)

B. The same procedure can be used with the following humorous nicknames for airlines collected by writer Peter S. Greenberg (S.F. Sunday Examiner and Chronicle, Sept. 2, 1985):

```
    o o o        o   o   .   o
1.  PAL      (Plane Always Late)
                           (Philippine Air Lines)


    o o o        o   o   o
2.  SAS      (Slow And Stop)
                           (Scandinavian Airlines)


    o o o        o   .   o   .   o   o
3.  TWA      (Teenie Weenie Airline)
             o   o   .   .   o
             (Try Walking Across)
                           (Trans World Airlines)


    o o o        o   o   .   o
4.  KLM      (Keep Loving Me)
                           (Royal Dutch Airlines)


    o o o        o   o   .   o   o
5.  PSA      (Poor Sailor's Airline)
                           (Pacific Southwest Airlines)


    o o o        o   o   .   .   o
6.  NWA      (Not Working Again)
                           (Northwest Airlines)
```

Reading Marked Syllable Length Exercise No. 2. Idioms serve as good texts for practice. Students are interested in learning idioms, and the rhythm of idioms
are conventionalized. Once students learn the rhythm
of an idiom, they can use it whenever they use the idiom. Two lists are given here. The first is a list of idioms
that students are likely to hear but are not advised to use
because they are too informal or because they are not yet
able to judge the appropriate settings in which they can
be used. The second list consists of idioms that they will
not only frequently hear but that nonnative speakers
can safely use as well. The division is subjective; the
point is that students should be aware of when, with
whom, and how these idioms may be used.

Read the following idioms to the students. Call their attention to the circles above the syllables of each word indicating syllable length. A dot represents a short syllable, and a circle represents a longer syllable. Elaborate on the idioms by creating an anecdote around them to illustrate their meanings. For example, for the first idiom, you would read it first and then illustrate it by saying something like, *Two students are talking about an exam they just took. Student A says, "That was the easiest exam Professor Higgins has ever given!" Student B replies, "Yeah, it was a piece of cake!"* Note that *of* should be pronounced as a schwa (/ /) or the idiom will sound odd.

A. Idioms for comprehension only:

    o . o . o
 1. It's a piece of cake.

    o o o o . . o .
 2. She got hot under the collar.

    o o . o
 3. Let's call it quits.

    o o . o
 4. You're off the hook.

    o o . o o
 5. Let's play it by ear.

B. Idioms that can be used:

    o . o o . . o .
 1. I'm a bit under the weather.

    o o . o o o . o .
 2. I need to pull myself together.

    o o . o . o . o . . . o .
 3. It's six of one and half a dozen of the other.

o o   o   o   o .   o
4. I just lost my train of thought.

o   o . o
5. Let's grab a bite.

After students have checked to see that they have marked the idioms correctly, they can practice saying them with a partner, who will be listening for the distinctions between long and short syllables.

For additional practice, pair students off and ask them to create a situation, two characters, and a conversation that at some point uses one of the idioms practiced.

Reading Marked Syllable Length Exercise No. 3. Read the following sentences and ask the students to notice the circles above the syllables of each word indicating syllable length. A dot represents a short syllable, and a circle represents a longer syllable.

                     o . . o . . . o .
1. *Question:* What is the capital of England?
                     o
   Answer: E.

                     o . . . o . . o .
2. *Question:* What is in the middle of Paris?
                     . o . o
   Answer: The letter r.

                     . . o . o . . o   o
3. *Question:* Do you stir your tea with your right hand
                     . .   o o
                or your left hand?

                     o o o o . . o
   Answer: I stir my tea with a spoon.

o o   o   .   o   . . o
4. *A:*   I just saw your name in a book!

o   o .   o   o
B: Oh, really? What book?

.   o   o
A: The phone book.

This time, ask the students to watch you as you read. Add a nonverbal gesture to coincide with each long syllable, for example, a slight nod of your head or a movement of your finger. The next time you read, have the students make some type of gesture for every long syllable they hear. Finally, ask the students to make these gestures simultaneously as they say the sentences. When students add these physical gestures, they get a better feeling for the variation in syllable length and the overall rhythm of sentences (Acton, personal communication; he has made kinesics, or body movements, a central part of his pronunciation instruction).

You might also select a videotape showing closeups of people speaking and have students observe their nonverbal behavior as a clue to rhythm. Turn off the sound so that the focus will be entirely on the visual images. In addition or alternatively, ask students to observe people outside of class: in the school cafeteria, on the bus, at the supermarket, on television.

Pauses and Thought Groups

Working on thought groups is a good way to help students whose tendency is to pronounce every syllable with equal length, giving listeners the impression that they are listening to a stream of syllables rather than groups of words. Begin by giving students texts with the thought groups already marked. Students should read each group as a unit and pause only at the end of each one. The pauses are important because their locations are determined by the grammar of English and are used by listeners to organize the information they hear. Each language uses pauses in accordance with its linguistic structure (Grosjean, 1980, cited in Gilbert, 1983). Moreover, some languages mark thought-group boundaries in other ways, such as with clause-final particles, and speakers of such languages would not think of using pauses for this purpose in English.

Exercises

Thought Groups Exercise No. 1

The juxtaposition of two prepositions in these sentences illustrates the importance of pausing to mark the boundary between phrases. Have the students listen as you read the sentences that follow and pause only at the point marked by a slash. Then have them practice in pairs with the listener monitoring for pauses only at the places marked.

1. What time do you come in/in the morning?

2. This is what I've been looking for/for hours!

3. Look your papers over/over the weekend.

4. Turn your papers in/in their final form on Monday.

5. Why don't you think it over/overnight?

You can follow up on this exercise by dividing the students into small groups to prepare a role play that they are free to improvise on any subject as long as they use these expressions in it.

Thought Groups Exercise No. 2

The following sentences illustrate the use of pauses

to separate lists of items. Follow the same procedure here as outlined for Exercise No. 1.

1. The three ages of man are:/ youth,/ middle age/ and "my how wonderful you look!"/

2. Puccini's opera "Turandot" requires three things: /big, thrilling voices,/ visual spectacle/ and orchestral sweep./

3. People are said to think,/ play/ and work at their best/ when the 24-hour temperatures/ average between 63 and 73 degrees Fahrenheit./

Complete this exercise with more sentences of this type that would best suit your students. After students have had practice pausing after items in a series, divide them into pairs or small groups. Ask them to interview one another using questions such as these:

1. If you had three wishes, what would they be?

2. If you could visit three cities (money is of no concern), what would they be?

3. When you came to the United States (or Canada, etc.), what were the three most essential items that you had to bring with you?

After the interviews have been completed, ask the students to report their results, taking care to pause after each item.

Thought Groups Exercise No. 3

The next set of sentences, all on the topic of contemporary superstitions and popular beliefs, illustrate the use of pauses to separate prepositional phrases and clauses. These sentences can be used with advanced level students; for students of intermediate proficiency, more appropriate sentences should be selected. Follow the same procedure for this exercise as outlined in Exercise No. 1.

1. In Illinois,/ driving around the house in low gear/ is said to cure a family member's illness./

2. In North Carolina,/ if the first bird seen on New Year's morning is flying high,/ there will be good health during the year./

3. Many superstitions follow the formula:/ if A/ then B/ with an optional C./

4. If you break a mirror,/ then you will have seven years' bad luck,/ unless you throw the broken pieces into a moving stream./

5. If you spill salt,/ then you will have bad luck,/ unless you throw some over your left shoulder./

Ask the students to discuss, in small groups, superstitions from their countries and then to report on their findings to the large group, monitoring themselves for placing pauses between phrases and clauses.

Thought Groups Exercise No. 4

These sentences all include a descriptive clause in the middle. Follow the procedure outlined in Exercise No. 1.

1. Folk beliefs and superstitions,/ which are found among people all over the world,/ provide a socially acceptable way for people to deal openly/ with frightening things that are not within their control./

2. Alan Dundes,/ who teaches folklore at the University of California, Berkeley,/ says that "it is a serious subject that deals with the essence of life."/

3. Scholars at the University of California at Los Angeles,/ who are compiling an encyclopedia of American superstitions and popular beliefs,/ have nearly one mil-

lion entries./

4. Many folk remedies contain a kernel of truth,/ as in the case of garlic,/ which has been found useful in treating hypertension./

5. Halloween,/ which in Europe honors the dead but in the United States celebrates childhood,/ points to the adoration of youth in America./

Ask the students to choose a subject, for example, their roommate, spouse, friend, or relative. Write two descriptive sentences about this person and then combine them into one sentence, making one an adjective clause. Ask the students to practice delivering the sentence with a partner, who will listen to check that the pauses are placed before and after the clause. Then ask the students to deliver their sentences to the class.

Thought Groups Exercise No. 5

Take a text that students might encounter on television or the radio. The following is the introduction to the television series, "The Twilight Zone." Have the students practice the introduction as though they were going to be the voice on television. Record their readings. Ask the students to watch the program, if available in your area, and compare their version with the one on television.

You're traveling through another dimension,/ a dimension not only of sight and sound/ but of mind;/ a journey into a wondrous land whose boundaries are that of the imagination./ That's the signpost up ahead/ . . . your next stop,/ the Twilight Zone./

Rhythm and Linking Sounds

Some students have learned English through the eye rather than through the ear, resulting in the false notion that words should be pronounced the way they look on the printed page, each one separated by blank spaces. Their speech typically is replete with pauses, one after every word. They need to learn to make smooth transitions from one word to the next. Other students have difficulty pronouncing consonants when they occur at the ends of words because consonants do not typically occur in this position in their native language. They, too, would benefit from attention to making transitions between words. For the latter, linking a final consonant sound to a beginning vowel sound alters the syllable structure from one that ends in a consonant to one that begins with one. For example, in the phrase *watch out,* if a speaker pronounced it as two separate words, both would be difficult because of the final consonant. But if the *ch* of *watch* is linked to the *ou* in *out*, it is no longer a final but an initial consonant in a now syllable, *chout*.

Exercises

Linking Sounds Exercise No. 1

Select common phrases that students are likely to hear. Pronounce them for the students, calling their attention to the way the final consonants of the first words are connected to the initial vowels of the second. Have the students practice saying them.

1. Look out!
2. Watch out!
3. Hurry up!
4. Thank you!
5. Not at all!

After students have practiced these phrases, briefly describe a situation to them and ask them to provide an appropriate response. For example, if you say, *You just opened the door for me and I said, "Thank you." What do you say?* the student would say *Not at all.* Here is another example: *You are waiting for a friend to go home. Your friend is putting her books away very slowly. What do you say?*

Linking Sounds Exercise No. 2

1. This little rhyme is a good example of how words can be restructured because of the way English links sounds of one word to the next:

> She was peeved and called him "Mr."
> Not because he went and kr.
>   But because just before,
>   As she opened the door,
> The same Mr. kr. sr.

Point out to the students how two words, *kissed her* can rhyme with one word, *mister* or *sister* in English. Give students time to practice saying this rhyme.

2. Students can also practice with the following rhyme, which also illustrates how sounds can cross word boundaries:

> Fuzzy Wuzzy was a bear
> Fuzzy Wuzzy had no hair
> Fuzzy Wuzzy wasn't fuzzy, was he?

Linking Sounds Exercise No. 3

These riddles in rhyme provide a humorous way to practice making links between words.

1. Brothers and sisters have I none,
   But that man's father was my father's son.
   (man looking at a picture of his son)

2. What's round like an apple,
   Shaped like a pear,

With a slit in the middle
All covered with hair? *(a peach)*

3. Round as an apple, flat as a hip,
Got two eyes and can't see a bit. *(a button)*

4. Walk on the living, they don't even mumble.
Walk on the dead, they grumble and grumble.
(leaves)

5. Comes in at every window
And every door crack,
Runs around and round the house
But never leaves a track.   *(the wind)*

Divide the students into groups of four or five. Have them practice these riddles in a round-robin fashion; that is, the first student to speak reads the first line; the next person takes the next, and so on. Group members should help each other remember to make the proper links between words (see Morley, forthcoming).

Linking Sounds Exercise No. 4

This exercise is for advanced students with enough experience listening to English to understand this conversation. It is taken from a comic strip called "The Born Loser" and starts out with two men with fishing poles on a pier. A third man arrives and starts talking to one of the men, while the other fishes and listens to their conversation with a quizzical expression. Students could first try to figure out what they are saying. Their conversation is written out the way it sounds. Alternatively, the teacher could read it to the students, who then try to write the conversation down in regular spelling.

Fisherman A: Hiya Mac.
Fisherman B: Lobuddy.
Fisherman A: Binear long?

Fisherman B:	Cuplours.
Fisherman A:	Ketchuneny?
Fisherman B:	Goddafew.
A:	Kindarthay?
B:	Bassencarp.
A:	Enysizetoum?
B:	Cuplapowns.
A:	Hittinard?
B:	Sordalite.
A:	Wahchoozin?
B:	Gobbawurms.
A:	Fishanonboddum?
B:	Rydonnaboddum.
A:	Goddago.
B:	Tubad. OK. Takideezy.
A:	Seeyarown. Gluk.
	(Addressing the third fisherman):
	Wahchooketchinfella?
C:	No entiendo senor.
A:	One other guy on the pier to talk to
	and he don't speak no English.

Here is the translation, just in case you'd like to check it out:

A:	Hiya Mac.
B:	Hello buddy.
A:	Been here long?
B:	Couple of hours.
A:	Catching any?
B:	Got a few.
A:	(What) kind are they?
B:	Bass and carp.
A:	Any size to them?
B:	Couple of pounds.
A:	Hitting hard?
B:	Sort of light.
A:	What are you using?
B:	(A) gob of worms.
A:	Fishing on the bottom?

B: Right on the bottom.
A: (I've) Got to go.
B: Too bad. OK. Take it easy.
A: See you around. Good luck.
B: What are you catching, fella?
C: *(Spanish for "I don't understand.")*

3
Intonation

What Is Intonation?

Like rhythm, intonation in English contributes to the structure and interpretation of information in speech. Whereas contrasting syllable length is the basis of rhythm, variations in pitch give form to intonation. Rises and falls in pitch are similar to those in music; in fact, intonation has been described as the melody of speech. These pitch rises and falls, when they serve to make something stand out as important, are referred to as accent here, following Bolinger (1981). While accent is an element of intonation, it is at the same time an element of rhythm because it also affects syllable length. Thus it is only for the convenience of discussion that rhythm and intonation have been separated. Activities described at the end of this chapter enable students ultimately to focus on both.

Intonation makes words stand out by creating peaks and valleys with pitch. Accenting a syllable with a high or a low pitch, compared with the pitch on the surrounding syllables, makes both the syllable and the word it is in more noticeable. This capability provides a speaker with a way to highlight certain information, because of its newness, informativeness, or interest, and backgrounding other information, because of its redundancy, lesser importance, or lack of interest. While speakers can choose which words to accent, English has a preference for peaks of prominence at the beginnings and ends of independent clauses, resulting in an intonation contour that looks like a suspension bridge:

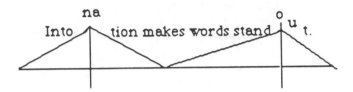

The peak at the beginning serves as an attention-getter, and the one at the end has the effect of a punch, suggests Bolinger (1981). What kinds of words do the accents tend to fall on? There seems to be a hierarchy with nouns at the top, followed by verbs; at the bottom are the function words: prepositions, pronouns, conjunctions, and articles.

Nonnative speakers who are unfamiliar with the way English uses pitch will often apply their native language rules to English. For example, in Tagalog, a word is emphasized by shifting its stressed syllable and lengthening the newly stressed syllable. We can see this rule being applied in the following statement made by a Filipino congressman: *This is an aMENDment to an aMENDment to an amendMENT* (Dacanay & Bowen, 1963). The stressed syllable, normally on the second syllable of *amendment,* is shifted by the Filipino speaker to the third syllable (the stressed syllables are represented in capital letters). If his intent was to emphasize the last *amendment,* it would be missed by the English speaker, who would expect the pitch to be most prominent on the second syllable of the third *amendment.* Just as speakers of other languages often apply native language intonation rules to English, English speakers approaching another language are likely to expect intonation to operate in the same way that it does in English. Learners of German, for example, may be surprised to find that the function of intonation in English to express shades of feelings is carried out in German by modal particles, such as *doch* and *etwa* (Schubiger, 1972). Another reason why nonnative speakers' accentual pattern may differ from that of English is that they may try to approximate the patterns of English. Consider this example: *Tonight we are going to sing a program of German SONGS, French SONGS, and Italian SONGS* (example from Davis, 1981). The speaker may have known that English uses stress but not how to choose the words to stress.

How can we teach learners to use intonation in English? Some simple rules have been formulated, which have been helpful for learners at the beginning stages. However, as they progress beyond this stage and encounter authentic speech samples, they find that these rules cannot be consistently applied. Take, for example, the rule that *wh*-questions are spoken with a terminal rising-falling intonation, as in:

What's for ^home^ work?

This rule implies that no other intonation pattern can be used with these types of questions, yet a rising intonation as in:

What's for home work?

is also possible and may be preferable in certain contexts, such as when the speaker wishes to appear nonchalant. Clearly, a description of intonation based solely on grammatical structure does not give learners sufficient information to discover what differences in intonation can mean.

A well-known rule states that the first member of a compound noun receives the stress, as in: *SUBway, STREETcar, HOMEwork, BLACKboard, CAble car,* and *PEAnut butter.* While this rule is descriptive, it requires elaboration. First of all, some noun compounds do not conform with this rule and receive stress on the second member. Consider these examples from Bolinger (1965): *lemon KISses* (compare with *LEmon drops*) and *hotel gaRAGE* (compare with *hoTEL room*) and *popuLAtion DENsity,* in which both nouns are stressed. Secondly, some noun compounds are stressed *and* accented and some are stressed but *not* accented. For example, consider the following sentences:

1. *(A student to the teacher, where* blackboard *is the focus word):*

I can't see the BLACKboard very well from here.

2. *(A teacher to the janitor, where* cleaning *is the focus word):*

The blackboard needs CLEANing.

In sentence (1), *blackboard* is accented, so accent and stress coincide. The first syllable is pronounced with either a high or low pitch and is also lengthened. In sentence (2), *blackboard* is not accented. The first syllable is stressed, but in this case there is no accompanying change in pitch, only a lengthening of the syllable.

Another familiar rule applies to noun phrases composed of an adjective and a noun, where the noun, being more important, will be accented, as in: *clean SHIRT, fast CARS, hot poTAto.* However, counterexamples can again be found to confuse the issue; compare the three phrases just cited with *TEE shirt, FAST pass* (the name of the bus pass offered by the San Francisco bus company), and *HOT dog.* Consider also these examples from Bolinger (1965): *a lean and HUNGry look; LEgal profession* versus *legal MARriage.* What needs to be added to the generalization about adjective + noun phrases is that as these phrases become more like nouns, they take on characteristics of nouns.

As with the noun compounds discussed earlier, these phrases also need to be examined in the context of sentences to see how accent affects intonation contours. Suppose two photographers are discussing the type of model they think would sell to advertisers:

A. Some magazines like to feature the lean and HUNGry look.

B. The lean and hungry look won't LAST.

Notice that the phrase *the lean and hungry look* is in a position favored to be accented, and the accent does occur on the stressable syllable of *hungry.* However, in B's response, since the idea of *lean and hungry* is no longer new information, it carries no accent, even though it is at the beginning of the sentence, a position also favored to be accented. The idea of the look's transitory nature is the piece of information that is new or important, so *last* is the word that is accented.

The stress patterns of compound nouns are vulnerable to a number of influences, as the history of the phrase *boy scouts* will illustrate. When the phrase first appeared, it could be pronounced *BOY scouts* or *boy SCOUTS,* like *boy KING* and *student PRINCE.* Then the scouts became institutionalized; other kinds of scouts faded from folklore; the girl scouts were organized and called *GIRL scouts* to contrast with *BOY scouts.* These developments, along with the analogy of forestress in other noun compounds, all figured in the fossilization of the accent on boy. Thus, the story of stress is not as simple and straightforward as it might appear.

These examples suggest that it is insufficient to teach students the conventions of noun and verb stress rules alone. Students need to learn how to determine what is considered common and redundant, and what is unusual and new. This knowledge can be applied more broadly than to just nouns and verbs. In a conversation, students need to learn how to acknowledge information given by their interlocutor in their responses. Otherwise, they will appear to be parrotting their conversational partner or ignoring what was said. Take for example this constructed interchange between a nonnative speaker and a supermarket clerk at the end of a sales transaction:

Clerk: THANK you.
NNS: THANK you.

An interchange between native speakers would transpire in this fashion:

Clerk: THANK you.
NS: Thank YOU.

Repeating the same accent pattern has the effect of seeming repetitive. In the second interchange, an accent on *you* acknowledges that the clerk has thanked the customer, who is returning the thanks. The next example of the need to use intonation in conversational dynamics comes from an observation of students reenacting a dialogue from a textbook.

Student A: What are you STUDying?
Student B: BUSiness. And what aBOUT you?

By not accenting *you,* student B fails to make the connection with student A's question and instead is asking a different, unrelated question on the order of *Tell me about yourself."*

In addition to structuring the way information is transferred from speaker to speaker, intonation cues listeners to the degree to which speakers may be controlling or revealing their emotions. An upward jump in pitch suggests that there is no restraint, while a downward jump suggests that there is. Consider this example from Bolinger (1972). Someone asks, "Why is it that you're willing to do business with Mary but not with me?" and the response is:

$$\text{Mary I can } ^{tr}{}^{u}\text{s}_{\text{t.}}$$

Mary is not accented to avoid being insultingly explicit about the contrast between *Mary* and *you,* as in the following:

$$\text{Ma}_{\text{ry I can}} {}^{tr}{}^{u}\text{s}_{\text{t.}}$$

A terminal falling intonation signals conclusiveness; the deeper the fall, the more conclusive the speaker is. In:

$$\text{Ab}_{\text{so}}{}^{\text{lute}}{}_{\text{ly}}$$

the speaker is not asking the listener for acceptance but is simply making a conclusive statement. Repeated accents in a sequence of single words create greater emphasis in a sentence than one with only two accents:

```
        ab   lute    pos
   I    so    ly        tive     wo
              i      ly      n't.
```

These generalizations of intonation are descriptively powerful, but they are not sufficiently detailed or comprehensive to equip a nonnative speaker with rules that can be applied in every context. The most productive approach to teaching intonation is, therefore, to provide speech samples that illustrate the dynamics of intonation and to teach students how to perceive them. The remainder of this chapter exemplifies ways to achieve these two objectives.

In order for students to learn to listen for intonation and begin to explore its functions, they need to start by learning to differentiate rising from falling pitch.

Teaching Students to Hear Pitch Changes

Before beginning intonation work, some preliminary exercises to focus students' attention on pitch are necessary because most people, native speakers of English included, are not accustomed to noticing pitch in language. The simplest task is to have students listen for the direction of pitch change in word-final position: rising or falling. The first exercise that follows, created by Allen (1971), serves this purpose.

Exercises

Listening for Pitch Changes Exercise No. 1

Record the following conversation and play it for the students. Establish the participants, the setting and the event by asking the students to guess who and what they are.

Conversation A

He: Ready? ↗
She: No. ↘
He: Why? ↘
She: Problems. ↘
He: Problems? ↗
She: Yes. ↘
He: What? ↘
She: Babysitter. ↘

The typical scenario that students come up with is as follows: A husband and wife are preparing to go out to a party or to dinner, but the babysitter has just phoned to say she could not make it, and so now they may not be able to go out after all. Another scenario proposed is that a young man has come to pick up his date, but she cannot go because the babysitter didn't show up, so she would have to stay home to babysit.

After the students have figured out what is going on, you can then play the conversation again. This time put the transcript of the conversation on the board or an overhead projector and ask the students to try to determine for each utterance whether the speaker's voice ends with a rising or a falling pitch. Students will be confused at first, especially with falling intonation on monosyllabic words; some students will identify these as rising. Draw arrows next to each utterance and play the conversation once more. To isolate pitch from the words, you can use a kazoo, which can be purchased at a toy store (see Gilbert, 1978). By humming into it, you can demonstrate rising and falling pitch to the amusement and illumination of your students. If your budget allows it, buy a kazoo for each student so they can all try it for themselves.

Ask the students to explain what each utterance means. Then point out that a change in pitch can indicate a change in meaning. *Ready?* with a rising pitch means, *Are you ready?* but *Ready* with a falling pitch means *I am ready. Why?* with a falling pitch means *I want a specific answer to my question,* while *Why?* with a rising pitch might mean *I want a specific answer to my question but I don't want to sound too insistent.*

Listening for Pitch Changes Exercise No. 2

List the following words on the board. Make your own list and mark the words for either a rise or fall in pitch. Read them one at a time as marked and ask students to point up if they hear a rise in pitch, down if they hear a fall. Confirm or inform their responses by marking the words on the board with an arrow pointing up or down.

↘ ready	↘ no
↗ problems	↗ yes
↗ babysitter	↗ no
↗ ready	↗ yes
↘ problems	↘ what
↘ yes	↗ why

Have the students pronounce each word with you, checking for the appropriate rise or fall in pitch.

Rising and Falling Pitch Exercise No. 1

Divide the students into pairs to practice the first conversation. Additional practice dialogues are provided here. Make up more for your particular students. Follow the procedure described for the first conversation, making sure the students know or have some idea of who is speaking, what the circumstances are, and what roles the speakers have in relation to one another.

Conversation B	**Conversation C**	**Conversation D**
A: Single?	A: Good?	A: Locked?
B: Double.	B: Delicious.	B: Locked.
A: Double?	A: More?	A: Key?

B: Yes.   B: Please.   B: Key?

A: Cone?   A: Key.

B: Cup.   B: Oh-oh.

Rising and Falling Pitch Exercise No. 2

This next exercise, a variation on the previous one, was created by Epstein (1983). Pair up students and give each pair an index card with the following instructions: "This conversation is out of order. Rearrange the sentences in the correct order on a separate piece of paper and mark the pitch as rising ↗ or falling ↘ ."

Here are some sample scrambled conversations. You can make up more of your own. Try unscrambling them yourself; some of them are not as easy as they appear.

Conversation #1	Conversation #2	Conversation #3
Sure.	Apple?	Five.
Cup of coffee?	Starved.	Please.
Milk?	Thanks.	Nonsmoking?
Pardon?	Hungry?	Reservations?
Black, please.	Sure?	This way.
Coffee?	Take it.	How many?
No.		

Once the students have unscrambled the phrases and marked the pitch patterns, give them time to practice. Then ask each pair to put their conversation on the board, explain the situation and perform it for the class. Other students can comment on the arrangement and propose other possibilities. The whole class can practice the final versions of each conversation.

Using Pitch
to Separate Phrases and Clauses

Besides the use of pauses to separate thought

daries. The arrows marked in the following texts show where there should be a slight rise in pitch. Ask the students to practice in pairs with the partners checking for these rises.

1. The three ages of man are:/ youth,/ middle age,/ and "my how wonderful you look!"/ ↘

2. Puccini's opera "Turandot" requires three things:/ big, thrilling voices,/ visual spectacle,/ and orchestral sweep./↘

3. People are said to think,/ play,/ and work at their best/ when the 24-hour temperatures/ average between 63 and 73 degrees Fahrenheit./

An introductory phrase or clause begins each of the next set of sentences. These are set off from the rest of each sentence by a rise-fall-rise pitch pattern.

1. In Illinois,/ driving around the house in low gear/ is said to cure a family member's illness.

2. In North Carolina,/ if the first bird seen on New Year's morning is flying high,/ there will be good health during the year./

3. If you break a mirror,/ then you will have seven years' bad luck,/unless you throw the broken pieces into a moving stream./

4. If you spill salt,/ then you will have bad luck,/ unless you throw some over your left shoulder./

In the final set of sentences, descriptive clauses come between the subject and the verb. The rise-fall-rise pitch pattern identifies the beginning and the end of these clauses, which contain information of secondary importance.

1. Folk beliefs and superstitions,/ which are found

among people all over the world,/ provide a socially
acceptable way for people to deal openly/ with
frightening things that are not within their control./

2. Alan Dundes,/ who teaches folklore at the University of California, Berkeley,/ says that "it is a serious
subject that deals with the essence of life."/

3. Scholars at the University of California at Los
Angeles,/ who are compiling an encyclopedia of American superstitions and popular beliefs,/ have nearly one
million entries./

Focus, Prominence, and Contrast

English uses pitch to signal the relative importance
of elements in discourse. Bolinger has described this
function as highlighting information with high pitch
and casting in shadow the rest of the information (cited
in Ladd, 1980). Words are made prominent by singling
out the stressed syllable of that word, raising or lower-
ing its pitch from a relatively constant pitch line, and as
a result drawing attention to that point. This property
also provides speakers with a device that can be used to
emphasize an idea, as well as to show contrast between
ideas.

Exercises

Focus, Prominence, and Contrast Exercise No. 1

This exercise illustrates how pitch and syllable
length work together to "put the spotlight" on information that is new, leaving in shadow what is not new or
redundant. The first conversation is from Allen (1971);
the rest follow the same model.

The accented syllables have been marked with a
large, clear circle, indicating length and also the posi-

tion where a change in pitch will occur. Record these conversations for playback in class or read them yourself. The advantage of recording them is that you can use two different voices in order to make it sound like a conversation. In addition, each playing will be uniform. (Reading the same text consistently with the same intonation each time is difficult, but can be done with practice.) Discuss with the class the reasons for highlighting the words in each conversation. Then give students a chance to practice taking both parts in each conversation.

Conversation A

A: I've lost an umbrella.
B: A lady's umbrella?
A: Yes. A lady's umbrella with stars on it. Green stars.

Conversation B

A: It's cold today.
B: It's not cold.
A: It is cold.
B: It isn't very cold.
A: It seems very cold.

Notice that in B's response, "It's not cold," *not* can be said with either a rising or a falling pitch. A rising pitch would sound more contradictory than a falling pitch.

Ask the students to decide which words should be highlighted in the next conversation.

Conversation C

A: Let's go out for dinner tonight.
B: O.K. What would you like to eat?
A: How about Arabic food?
B: I know a good restaurant on Fifth Avenue. It's inexpensive and not far from here.
A: That sounds good.

A number of systems have been used to represent the rise and fall in pitch, among them lines, musical notations, and rearranging the letters on the page to correspond with the pitch direction. Of these methods, the last seems to be the easiest for students, and teachers, to understand. Try reading these:

Conversation A:

A: I've lost an um ^{brel} la.

B: A la$^{dy's}$ umbrella?

A: $^Y_{e}$s. A lady's umbrella with ^{stars} on it.

Green $_{stars}$.

Conversation B:

A: It's ^{cold} today.

B: It's $_{not}$ cold.

A: It ^{is} cold.

B: It isn't $_{very}$ cold.

A: It ^{seems} very cold.

Focus, Prominence, and Contrast Exercise No. 2

Record these sentences to show how the informativeness or redundancy principle works with accents on noun compounds. When they refer to new information, the accent falls on the first noun, but when they contain old information, the accent moves to a point of new focus. After students have studied these noun compounds in accented and unaccented positions, ask them to read these sentences. The capital letters identify the syllables that that are accented. The circles serve as reminders that these syllables should be long. Where circles and capitalized words coincide, students should make an effort to lengthen the syllables and raise the pitch over these syllables.

1. *(an excerpt from a weather report):* A HEAT wave hit the area yesterday. . . .
   The heat wave sent record crowds to the areas PARKS.

2. A: What are you looking for?
   B: My CHECKbook.
   A: The only checkbook on the desk is MINE.

3. *(Two friends have just gotten into a car.)*
   A: You have to put on your SEATbelt.
   B: Must I? I HATE wearing seatbelts.
   A: I'm afraid it's the LAW.

Create more contexts of your own like these. They're not difficult to do. When you start looking, you'll find noun compounds everywhere.

Focus, Prominence, and Contrast Exercise No. 3

Cartoons and magazine ads are rich sources of examples of accent used to show contrast. If they are in black and white, they can be easily made into transparencies and projected for the whole class to look at and work on together. Students can look at the picture, discuss what the situation is, then decide how to mark and read the sentence(s). The following examples are already marked.

1. *(The cat Garfield and his human companion Jon are on their hands and knees observing an army of ants.)*

Jon: There must be MILLions of ants down there. I wonder how you tell the difference between BOY ants and GIRL ants.

Garfield: I guess THEY didn't have any trouble figuring it out.

Because the two characters are looking at the ants, they would not accent *ants* because it is not a new idea. The focus of attention is on the numbers. The second sentence illustrates how accent is used to show contrast between *boy ants* and *girl ants.* The accent on *they* in the final sentence relates Garfield's statement to Jon's, implying that even though Jon couldn't figure out the difference, the ants could.

2. *(Mrs. Lockhorn has opened a gift given to her by her husband.)* I said MINK coat, not PINK coat.

In a noncontrastive statement, such as *My husband bought me a pink COAT,* the accent would be on *coat,* the favored word for accent in a favored position for accent. Shifting the accent to *pink,* therefore, calls attention to it.

3. *(A teacher is standing at the blackboard with a student who has written: 2+2= 5.)* Now suppose you give us the answer withOUT inflation.

Recall that prepositions are at the bottom of the hierarchy of accentable words. As a result, accenting prepositions call attention to them.

4. *(A little boy is sad because his neighbor and good friend Lawrence has moved.)*

Boy: Lawrence is gone, isn't he?
Mother: Yes, they left early this morning.
Boy: I just saw their house—it's empty. Mom, how long will I feel empty, too?

Unless pronouns appear at the beginnings of sentences, they are also at the bottom of the hierarchy of accentable words. Thus, accenting them calls attention to them.

5. *(Charlie Brown is talking to Lucy.)*

Charlie Brown: I want to be liked for mySELF, I don't want to be liked because I know the right PEOple. I want to be liked for ME.

      Lucy: WHO?

The same comment made about item No. 4 applies here.

Summary Exercises

These exercises provide students with an opportunity to review the principles of (a) pauses to mark thought groups, (b) rising pitch at the ends of phrases to mark thought groups, (c) accents to highlight, focus or contrast information, (d) the use of low pitch to play down information. Select texts that have built-in reasons for rehearsals: telling jokes and anecdotes; performing scenes from plays; filming a commercial or news broadcast; giving a formal presentation. Following are suggestions for each of these.

A. Record the following jokes. The first set consists of shorter texts than the second. Before playing them, ask the students to mark: (a) where they think the pauses should go and (2) which words should be highlighted. Students can then check their guesses against the recorded version. Discuss their choices and help them puzzle out their questions. A copy of these texts marked for intonation is in Appendix B.

1. The teacher asked a student, "John, name two pronouns." John, who suddenly woke up, said, "Who, me?"

2. The teacher said, "Today, we will review our tenses. Now, if I say, 'I am beautiful,' what tense is it?" A student replied, "Obviously the past tense."

3. A drunk walked up to a man and asked, "What

time is it?" The man said, "It's 11 o'clock." The drunk said, "I must be going crazy. All day long I keep getting different answers."

4. "We have everything on the menu today, sir," the waiter said. "So I see," said the customer. "May I have a clean one?"

5. A woman was standing on a railroad platform and overheard a man asking for a round-trip ticket. "To where?" asked the ticket agent. "To here, of course," replied the man.

6. "Those people upstairs are very annoying," complained the tenant. "Last night they stomped and banged on the floor until midnight." "Did they wake you?" asked the landlord. "No," replied the tenant. "Luckily, I was playing my tuba."

B. Examine the following anecdote. In telling the anecdote, which words would be important for your listeners to hear and understand? In a small group, discuss which words these might be and underline them. Check your guesses with your teacher. Then mark the stressed syllable of words that have more than one syllable. Next, mark the phrase boundaries. Mark all of the syllables for length, using the system of dots and circles. (Advanced students can also mark intonation lines; or they can practice reading the texts according to the way they have been marked in Appendix B.) Practice telling this anecdote. Each person in your group should say one phrase; the next person would then continue with the next phrase. Take turns in this fashion until the end of the anecdote. This turn-taking system is called a round robin.

A businessman went to a psychiatrist and said, "Doctor, I don't know what's wrong with me. Nobody wants to talk to me. My employees don't talk to me; my children don't talk to me; my wife doesn't talk to me. Why is it that nobody wants to talk to me?" The psychiatrist's response was, "Next!"

Each group will receive a different anecdote. Follow the same procedure with this anecdote as you did with the example. After you have practiced telling the anecdote in a round robin, tell it to the rest of the class.

1. A traveler stopped at a historic hotel and requested the rates for a single room. "A room on the first floor is $100, on the second floor $80, and on the third floor $60," replied the desk clerk. The traveler thought a bit, said thank you and turned to go. "Don't you like our hotel?" asked the clerk. "Oh, it's beautiful," said the traveler. "It just isn't tall enough."

2. Three men were in a hospital waiting room when a nurse rushed in and said to the first man, "Sir, you're the father of twins." "That's a coincidence," he said. "I'm a member of the Minnesota Twins."

Later, the nurse returned and said to the second man, "Sir, you're the father of triplets!" "Another coincidence!" the second man said, "I'm with the 3M Company!"

The third man jumped to his feet, grabbed his hat and said, "I'm getting out of here. I work for 7 Up!"

3. We take the bus to school every day, and every morning as soon as the bus reaches the campus, everybody rushes to get off. One day, one of the first students to get off suddenly turned around and tried to get back on. He was having a hard time and started shouting, "My lunch! My lunch!" A voice from the back of the bus answered, "It was delicious!"

4. The wife of a foreign graduate student could not speak a word of English and so was terrified every time the telephone rang when her husband was not at home. He taught her to say, "Mr. Montoya is not at home." But this didn't help much because the caller usually continued talking. He then taught her to add, "He will be back this afternoon." Her problem was still unsolved because callers sometimes left messages she couldn't understand. Finally, the couple figured out a solution. When the phone rang, Mrs. Montoya answered, "Mr. Montoya is not at home. He will be back this afternoon.

This is a recording."

5. A friend of ours had to call a plumber recently to fix a broken faucet. The job didn't take long. When he finished, he gave her the bill. When she saw what he charged her for five minutes of work, she was shocked. "Your prices are very high, aren't they?" she said to him. "Do you know the doctor costs less than this when he makes a house call?" "I know," answered the plumber. "I was a doctor until I was lucky enough to find this job a few months ago."

6. The Browns recently moved into a new house. One Saturday, the father took his car out of the garage and was washing it when a neighbor came by. The neighbor stopped and commented, "That's a nice car. Is it yours?" "Sometimes," the father answered. The neighbor was surprised. "Sometimes?" he said. "What do you mean?" "Well," the father answered, "when there's a party, it belongs to my daughter. When there's a football game, it belongs to my son. When I've washed the car and it looks really nice and clean, it belongs to my wife. And when it needs gas, it's mine."

7. A doctor had an elderly patient, Mr. Peterson, who had to be hospitalized. On the first morning, he went to see Mr. Peterson and said, "Mr. Peterson, you're going to get some injections and then you'll feel much better. A nurse will come and give you the first one this morning and then you'll get another one this evening." A few minutes later, a young nurse came to Mr. Peterson's bed and said to him, "I'm going to give you the first injection now, Mr. Peterson. Where do you want it?" Mr. Peterson was surprised. He looked at the nurse for a moment and then said, "Nobody's ever let me choose before. Are you really going to let me choose now?" "Yes, Mr. Peterson," the nurse answered impatiently. "Where do you want it?" "Well, then," Mr. Peterson answered with a smile, "I want it in *your* left arm, please."

Many of these anecdotes come from 20 years of *Reader's Digest*.

C. Rehearsing and performing excerpts from carefully selected dramatic works is another way to review rhythm and intonation and to develop the students' sense of how these features are exploited to communicate meaning. To be an effective exercise, it is important that students understand the drama, whether it is a play or a screenplay. Seeing it performed in a theater or on screen before attempting to perform it is an essential preliminary step. The objective here is not to put on a performance but to give students a context within which to explore the mechanisms of rhythm and intonation. The involvement that an interesting play or screenplay can engender also fuels students' motivation to focus on rhythm and intonation, making this project well worth the effort. If possible, videotape the performance so that students have a concrete goal to work toward and will be able to view and evaluate their own efforts.

In choosing plays, look for ones that have dialogue that students can understand and potentially use. Find scenes that involve two characters that the students would not be embarrassed to play. The dialogue for each character should be balanced, so that one character is not doing all the talking. In this way, the class can be divided into pairs with every pair working on the same scene. This allows everyone to analyze the same text for rhythm and intonation and to compare the attempts to exploit them in their performances. The following plays fit these criteria and are tried and true:

"Ah, Wilderness" by Eugene O'Neill;
"Arsenic and Old Lace" by Joseph Kesselring;
"I Remember Mama" by John van Druten;
"Our Town" by Thornton Wilder; and
"Dial 'M' for Murder" by Frederick Knott.

Copies of these plays can be ordered from the Drama Book Shop, 150 W. 52nd St., New York, NY 10019. For other play suggestions, consult Richard Via's *English in Three Acts*.

D. The final suggestion for a review activity is to

have students prepare a 3-5 minute presentation in writing, but in a spoken style. This presentation will be recorded so that both you and the student can participate in its evaluation. Students should be told at the beginning that this assignment will culminate the course. It provides a concrete goal for them to work toward and helps to motivate them to develop the clearest pronunciation they can. Following is a suggested procedure for carrying out this final activity.

First edit the students' text for grammar. Then ask the students to mark the text for the following:

- thought groups;
- key words to be highlighted;
- key words that should be linked (for example, words that end in *s*);
- key words' syllable length;
- intonation at the ends of phrases, clauses, lists; and
- adjective clauses (practice saying them with low pitch).

Have students practice their presentations using the read-and-look-up method (as described on p. 00). Then have them record the presentation on tape at home to turn in, or make the presentation in class and record it simultaneously. The latter choice is preferable since true communication requires an audience that offers feedback that would not be available otherwise.

Concluding Remarks

This monograph should serve as a guide for teachers in assessing the pronunciation needs of their students and in planning an appropriate instructional program for them. The emphasis here has been on the major elements of spoken English that affect communicative effectiveness the most: rhythm and intonation. Individual sounds have been treated only insofar as they relate to rhythm and intonation. Although much of rhythm and intonation remains undescribed here, the approach to teaching pronunciation advocated here has not relied on a comprehensive description;

rather, the focus has been on providing learners with the perceptive skills and sufficient data with which to discover aspects of the system on their own. For teachers new to teaching pronunciation, this process is likely to be one that they will share with their students. May it be a rich and rewarding process for all.

References

Acton, W. (1984). Attending skills for ESL students. *American Language Journal 2(2)*, 17-37.

Allen, V.F. (1971). Teaching intonation, from theory to practice. *TESOL Quarterly, 5*, 73-81.

Beebe, L. (1983). Risk-taking and the language learner. In H. Seliger & M. Long (Eds.), *Classroom oriented research in second language acquisition*. Rowley, MA: Newbury House.

Bolinger, D. (1965). Stress and information. In I. Abe & T. Kanekiyo (Eds.), *Forms of English*. Cambridge, MA: Harvard University Press. Originally published in *American Speech, 33*, 5-20 (1958).

Bolinger, D. (1965). Contrastive accent and contrastive stress. In I. Abe & T. Kanekiyo (Eds.), *Forms of English*. Cambridge, MA: Harvard University Press. Originally published in *Language, 37*, 83-96 (1961).

Bolinger, D. (1972). Around the edge of language: Intonation. In D. Bolinger (Ed.), *Intonation: Selected readings*. Harmondsworth, U.K.: Penguin Books. Originally published in *Harvard Educational Review 34(2)*: 282-93 (1964).

Bolinger, D. (1981). *Two kinds of vowels, two kinds of rhythm*. Bloomington, IN: Indiana University Linguistics Club.

Bolinger, D. (1985). Two views of accent. *Journal of Linguistics, 21,* 79-123.

Bowen, D. (1972). Contextualizing pronunciation practice in the ESOL classroom. *TESOL Quarterly, 6*(1), 83-94.

Brown, G. (1977). *Listening to spoken English.* London: Longman.

Celce-Murcia, M. (1983). Activities for teaching pronunciation communicatively. *CATESOL News*, May 1983, *10.*

Chan, M. (n.d.). *Your attention, please! Improving conversation skills through active listening.* Unpublished manuscript.

Dacanay, F.R., & Bowen, J.D. (1963). *Techniques and procedures in second language teaching.* Quezon City, The Philippines: Alemar-Phoenix Publishing House.

Davis, C. (1981). Report of "Rhythm, stress and intonation" by W. Jones, *JALT Newsletter, 5,* 12.

Epstein, J. (1983). Intonation. *CATESOL News.* December 1983, 7.

Gilbert, J. (1978). Gadgets: Nonverbal tools for teaching pronunciation. *CATESOL Occasional Papers ,4,* 68-78.

Gilbert, J. (1983). Pronunciation and listening comprehension. *Cross Currents, 10*(1), 53-61.

Gilbert, J. (1984). *Clear speech.* Cambridge, MA: Cambridge University Press.

Ladd, D.R., Jr. (1980). *The structure of intonational meaning.* Bloomington, IN: Indiana University Press.

Leather, J. (1985). Second-language pronunciation learning and teaching. In V. Kinsella (Ed.), *Cambridge Language Teaching Survey 3.* Cambridge, MA: Cambridge University Press.

Morley, J. (1979). *Improving spoken English.* Ann Arbor, MI: The University of Michigan Press.

Morley, J. (forthcoming). *Principles, techniques, and activities for teaching pronunciation.* New York: Oxford University Press.

Pennington, M., & Richards, J.C. (1986). Pronunciation revisited. *TESOL Quarterly 20*(2), 207-226.

Prator, C., & Robinett, B. (1985). *Manual of American English pronunciation.* New York: Holt, Rinehart and Winston.

Richards, J.C., & Bycina, D. (1984). *Person to person.* New York: Oxford University Press.

Savignon, S. (1983). *Communicative competence: Theory and classroom practice.* Reading, MA: Addison-Wesley.

Schubiger, M. (1972). English intonation and German modal particles: A comparative study. In D. Bolinger (Ed.), *Intonation.* Harmondsworth, U.K.: Penguin Books. Originally published in *Phonetica, 12,* 65-84 (1965).

Via, R. (1976). *English in three acts.* The University Press of Hawaii.

Wong, R. (1986). Does pronunciation teaching have a place in the communicative language classroom? In D. Tannen & J. Alatis (Eds.), *GURT '85, Languages and linguistics: The interdependence of theory, data, and application.* Washington, DC: Georgetown University Press.

Appendix A

Speech Diagnostic Checklist

1. Thought groups are difficult to identify; pauses occur between almost every word, instead of groups of words.

2. Rhythm distorted because of little or no linking.

3. No differentiation of syllable length.

4. Reduced vowels are pronounced as full vowels.

5. Vowels before voiced consonants are not lengthened.

6. Words in phrases are undistinguished; no word can be singled out as most prominent.

7. The wrong word is accented in sentences.

8. Stress is on the wrong syllable of polysyllabic words.

9. Syllables are deleted from some words.

10. Vowel deleted from syllables.

11. Consonant deleted from syllables.

12. Vowel inserted into syllable.

13. Consonant inserted into syllable.

14. Wrong word accented in sentences.

15. Too many accented words in sentence.

16. A rise in pitch was used instead of a fall.

17. A fall in pitch was used instead of a rise.

Sample Texts Marked for Intonation

Intonation can be shown by arranging the letters to correspond with a rise or fall in pitch as in the following example.

1. The ^{tea}cher asked a student,/ Joh^n/ name ^{two} pronouns/

^{Jo}h^n/ who suddenly woke u^{p}/ said/ W$_{ho}$/ m^{e}/

Alternatively, the rises and falls can be indicated with horizontal and vertical lines as the following examples illustrate. Of course, other choices of accents and pitch patterns are possible, but what is important is that the marking system represent what the students actually hear. In order to use this system, teachers will need to spend time learning it, so that they can read the sentences in the same way each time.

1. The teacher asked a student, "John, name two pronouns." John, who suddenly woke up, said, "Who,

me?"

2. The teacher said, "Today, we will review our tenses. Now, if I say, 'I am beautiful,' what tense is it?" A student replied, "Obviously the past tense."

3. A drunk walked up to a man and asked, "What time is it?" The man said, "It's 11 o'clock." The drunk said, "I must be going crazy. All day long I keep getting different answers."

4. "We have everything on the menu today, sir," the waiter said. "So I see," said the customer. "May I have a clean one?"

5. A woman was standing on a railroad platform and overheard a man asking for a round-trip ticket. "To where?" asked the ticket agent. "To here, of course," replied the man.

6. "Those people upstairs are very annoying," complained the tenant. "Last night they stomped and banged on the floor until midnight." "Did they wake you?" asked the landlord. "No," replied the tenant. "Luckily, I was playing my tuba."

7. A businessman went to a psychiatrist and said, "Doctor, I don't know what's wrong with me. Nobody wants to talk to me. My employees don't talk to me; my

children don't talk to me; my wife doesn't talk to me. Why is it that nobody wants to talk to me?" The psychiatrist's response was, "Next!"

8. A traveler stopped at a historic hotel and requested the rates for a single room. "A room on the first floor is $100, on the second floor $80, and on the third floor $60," replied the desk clerk. The traveler thought a bit, said "Thank you" and turned to go. "Don't you like our hotel?" asked the clerk. "Oh, it's beautiful," said the traveler. "It just isn't tall enough."

9. Three men were in a hospital waiting room when a nurse rushed in and said to the first man, "Sir, you're the father of twins." "That's a coincidence," he said. "I'm a member of the Minnesota Twins." Later, the nurse returned and said to the second man, "Sir, you're the father of triplets!" "Another coincidence!" the second man said, "I'm with the 3M Company!" The third man jumped to his feet, grabbed his hat and said, "I'm getting out of here. I work for 7 Up!"

10. We take the bus to school every day and every morning as soon as the bus reaches the campus, everybody rushes to get off. One day, one of the first students to get off suddenly turned around and tried to get back on. He was having a hard time and started shouting, "My lunch! My lunch!" A voice from the back of the bus answered, "It was delicious!"

11.   The wife of a foreign graduate student could not speak a word of English and so was terrified every time the telephone rang when her husband was not at home. He taught her to say, "Mr. Montoya is not at home." But this didn't help much because the caller usually continued talking. He then taught her to add, "He will be back this afternoon." Her problem was still unsolved because callers sometimes left messages she couldn't understand. Finally, the couple figured out a solution. When the phone rang, Mrs. Montoya answered, "Mr. Montoya is not at home. He will be back this afternoon. This is a recording."

12.   A friend of ours had to call a plumber recently to fix a broken faucet. The job didn't take long. When he finished, he gave her the bill. When she saw what he had charged her for 5 minutes of work, she was shocked. "Your prices are very high, aren't they?" she said to him. "Do you know the doctor costs less than this when he makes a house call?" "I know," answered the plumber. "I was a doctor until I was lucky enough to find this job a few months ago."

13.   The Browns recently moved into a new house. One Saturday, the father took his car out of the garage and was washing it when a neighbor came by. The neighbor stopped and commented, "That's a nice car. Is it yours?" "Sometimes," the father answered. The neighbor was surprised. "Sometimes?" he said. "What

do you mean?" "Well," the father answered, "when there's a party, it belongs to my daughter. When there's a football game, it belongs to my son. When I've washed the car and it looks really nice and clean, it belongs to my wife. And when it needs gas, it's mine."

14. A doctor had an elderly patient, Mr. Peterson, who had to be hospitalized. On the first morning, he went to see Mr. Peterson and said, "Mr. Peterson, you're going to get some injections and then you'll feel much better. A nurse will come and give you the first one this morning and then you'll get another one this evening." A few minutes later, a young nurse came to Mr. Peterson's bed and said to him, "I'm going to give you the first injection now, Mr. Peterson. Where do you want it?" Mr. Peterson was surprised. He looked at the nurse for a moment and then said, "Nobody's ever let me choose before. Are you really going to let me choose now?" "Yes, Mr. Peterson," the nurse answered impatiently. "Where do you want it?" "Well, then," Mr. Peterson answered with a smile, "I want it in your left arm, please."

About the Author

Rita Wong has taught in a variety of educational settings: junior high school, adult education, intensive English, continuing education, corporate, and university degree programs. As a teacher trainer, she has taught methodology courses in master's degree as well as certificate programs and conducted workshops on teaching pronunciation and other skills in North America and abroad. She is an active member of TESOL and CATESOL, the California Teachers of English to Speakers of Other Languages, which she has served as secretary, newsletter editor, vice president (1985-86) and president in 1986-87. She is currently assistant director of the American Language Institute at San Francisco State University, where she also coordinates their oral communication and listening comprehension skills courses.